TRAUMA-ORGANIZED SYSTEMS

Other titles in the

Systemic Thinking and Practice Series

edited by David Campbell & Ros Draper
published and distributed by Karnac Books

Credit Card orders, Tel: 0171-584-3303; Fax: 0171-823-7743

TRAUMA-ORGANIZED SYSTEMS

Physical and Sexual Abuse in Families

REVISED EDITION

Arnon Bentovim

Foreword by
Donald A. Bloch

Systemic Thinking and Practice Series

Series Editors
David Campbell & Ros Draper

London
KARNAC BOOKS

First published in 1992 by
H. Karnac (Books) Ltd.
58 Gloucester Road
London SW7 4QY

This edition published
with revisions in 1995

British Library Cataloguing in Publication Data

Bentovim, Arnon
   Trauma-organized Systems: Physical and
   Sexual Abuse in Families. — (Systemic
   Thinking & Practice Series)
   I. Title   II. Series
   155.232

ISBN 1 85575 012 0

ACKNOWLEDGEMENTS

Although I was the consultant responsible for the cases referred to, the interviews and sessions described to illustrate the ideas were the work of myself and my colleagues.

I acknowledge them, and the individuals and families we worked with, as my sources of inspiration with much gratitude. They include Marianne Tranter, Barbara Segal, Jill Hodges, and Joanne Sylvester. I am also grateful to David Campbell and Ros Draper for their continuing encouragement.

CONTENTS

EDITORS' FOREWORD

With this book, more than any other in our series, we have had the practitioner in mind. Practitioners dealing with child abuse, sexual abuse, or family violence are frequently at the edge of their own emotional and intellectual capacity. "How can people do these things?" "Where is the possible meaning in all this?" "Can I bear the emotional impact of working on this case?" These are all questions we have heard people asking about this work, and we believe this area of work requires models and frameworks for thinking that the practitioner can use to make some sense of the highly complex and highly emotive issues involved. A useful way of conceptualizing helps to manage the powerful feelings that are stirred up in everyone who gets involved in these cases.

The concept of the trauma-organized system allows workers to think about the way events are connected at many different levels, from the individual, to the familial, to the professional, and beyond to the societal and cultural levels. By seeing things in a coherent framework, it makes it easier to plan appropriate interventions. The book describes ways in which interventions can be made at different levels of this system, and it outlines various treatment approaches, such as group work for victims and perpetrators, marital and family therapy, and individual work. The book also contains a very helpful introduction in which Bentovim, who is a very experienced practitioner in this field, describes the way his thinking has changed recently with the impact of feminist thinking and constructivism.

Readers may feel challenged about their own positions in the trauma-organized system (we hope they will), but the challenge also leads to new ways of thinking which can stimulate the professional worker to create effective manoeuvrability within these complicated systems.

David Campbell
Ros Draper
London
October 1992

FOREWORD

Donald A. Bloch

There are no problems as challenging for family systems therapists as the treatment of abusive families. Chief among the difficulties is that the ordinary therapeutic stance of neutrality and even-handed attention to the needs and concerns of every family member cannot, by itself, be effective in most of these instances. Multiple frames of reference inform the definition of the problem; they are often in conflict with each other. The therapist (or the therapy team) must operate with a clear understanding of the power position of women and children relative to men in our society, about the ubiquity of violence in human interactions. The blurred outlines of generational boundaries need to be delineated in situations where the landscape is not always clearly marked. The rights of individuals must be balanced against those of the group, often by invoking the police power of society as part of the therapeutic group.

The ground is treacherous, and we all must sail between the Scylla of denial and complicitous permissiveness on the one hand, and the Charybdis of self-righteousness on the other. We cannot afford to confuse social control with punitiveness, or clear boundary definition with vengeful retribution.

Many different kinds of families are described as violent and abusive. In all of them, the common thread is that the powerless are mistreated, that the normal protectiveness one would expect to find towards those who are vulnerable by virtue of age or gender (the young and the aged), does not get invoked, and in fact, that the reverse is true.

The traditional protected stance of the therapist simply will not do in these situations. The therapist (or the therapy team), must often be pro-active and confrontational in the treatment encounter itself.

Arnon Bentovim writes from deep clinical wisdom and honestly appraised experience with a wide variety of violent family situations. He recognizes how intractable many of these patterns are, yet he is cautiously optimistic (recidivism rates are between 30 and 60%). His optimism seems solidly based on an understanding of what kind of people are more likely to be abusers ("impulsive, immature, and prone to depression") and on the notion that "stable, global negative attributions exist about children and partners who are subsequently victimized, which predispose to grievance and anger". Violence seems to occur where alternatives are not possible.

According to Arnon Bentovim, ". . . a key element is the attachment pattern between parent and child." Several patterns of insecure attachment are described: avoidant, re-enacting or reversing, and disorganized (punishment is justified to gain some measure of control).

In sexual victimizing patterns two major factors are described: the substitution of sexual responses for normal affectionate contact, and the use of sexual victimizing responses to assert power and control, what the author calls the "sexualization of interpersonal relations" and the "sexualization of subordination".

Bentovim offers a conceptual frame and specific treatment advice. His main orientation is ". . . to see victimizing actions and traumatic effects as the elements of the 'trauma-organized system' "—"The essence of trauma-organized systems is that they are focused on *action*, not *talking* or *thinking*." Victimizing activities are justified by construing some action or aspect of the victim as causal.

This puts the matter under the general class of problem-determined or problem-organized systems, giving full weight to the part societal definitions play in creating and maintaining these patterns.

An important aspect of this view is that treating agencies must be factored into understanding both the problem and the solution.

I am particularly pleased at the author's use of social constructivist concepts in his work. By helping victim and perpetrator alike to re-story their experience there is the possibility for moving forward from these grim, repetitive, stuck cycles of interaction. And there is the sad acknowledgement that on some occasions the crime is too monstrous to allow it to be accepted by the perpetrator.

There are no human situations more desperate and more cruel. Carlos Sluzki, commenting on the connection between political torture and family violence, has noted how, in both instances, the true evil lies in that the helpless are harmed by the very agencies most obligated to protect them—the government and the family. As therapists struggle to meet this challenge, they will receive much useful help from this book.

August 1992

Why attempt to develop a systemic approach to family violence?

One of the most powerful issues to have affected the family therapy field in recent years has been the realization that inequalities and violations are an inherent part of family life. Familiar notions and pre-suppositions in family therapy which see members of a family having an equal contribution to a system are being challenged. Ideas that have been part of my own practice since I began to use a family therapy approach in the late 1960s are being questioned.

From a feminist gender-based perspective, violence, incest, and other forms of intra-familial violence are not being seen as a symptom of a malfunctioning family but as a social and political problem stemming from a patriarchal society's inability to protect victims. Incest, spouse abuse, child abuse are viewed as coercive acts performed by men to control and subordinate spouses and children, and as an organizing force behind the family's patterns of interaction. The accusation is put forward that family therapists lose sight of the power of abusive and incestuous acts and of their ramifications for victims. It is also argued that a neutral stance giving apparent equal attention to all family members may tacitly approve and encourage the very behaviour the therapist is trying to change.

Accusations are made that conjoint family work may be detrimental to victims because the approach implies that all family members, including the victim, play a role in maintaining abusive interactions. Power imbalances that are part of the family are therefore perpetuated in the therapy room: the status quo is maintained.

This has led to forceful views being advanced about ways of working with family violence. Violent men need to be worked with in their own right; abused children and women need appropriate societal protection, not to be thrust into the family arena until there has been real evidence of change. The challenge to family therapists has, of course, been profound. Attempts have been made to introduce a feminist-informed family approach (Barrett, Trepper, & Fish, 1990). This advocates different ways of equalizing power, ending denial of the abuse, and ensuring victims are protected and extracted from victim roles and empowered and helped to make better relationships, impacting as much as possible on traditional sex-roled relationships. There have recently been attempts by the Ackerman Group (Goldner, Penn, Sheinberg, & Walker, 1990) to apply some new ways of thinking about gender, to bring together the strength of family approaches, with sensitivity towards gender and power differentials.

There is currently a broad concern with issues of social justice and the way such issues as poverty and race impact on family life and relationships. Family therapists have had to look critically at issues of power, considering those practices that we have used to empower parents to take control of their children and asking whether these may be abusive rather than reorganizing.

My own practice since the late 1960s has always had a dual thrust, on the one hand working with general family problems presenting through child or adult, and, on the other, working with abused children and their families. My approach to family work has always linked dynamic thinking with systems notions. "Focal" family therapy has been the overall framework developed with my colleagues at Great Ormond Street, with much work being done in conjunction with Warren Kinston (Bentovim & Kinston, 1991). This has paid attention to the way early stressful and traumatic events are processed, the way they affect family life, and how to use the powerful interventions developed by family therapists to achieve change.

My work with child abuse over the same period has been concerned with child, family, and professional systems, in hospitals,
Social Service departments, and the courts. As well as providing
treatment services, diagnostic and management approaches have
been important, with child protection as a key issue. In the development of a child sexual abuse treatment service, it proved more possible to link family therapy ideas with the abuse field. The period in
which our sexual abuse work developed (1980 to the present) has
also coincided with major controversies in the field: the renewed
debate about "power" as a reality—which is Haley's view—and
Bateson's view of power as "A Tragic Epistemological Error" (Dell,
1989).

The controversy about "neutrality" as being implicitly supportive of the status quo has been fiercely advanced. My own attempts
at describing our sexual abuse work in systemic terms has been
criticized. It has been argued that any family work that involved
abusive fathers could be seen as minimizing abusive actions, thus
putting the children at risk of re-abuse.

As a result I have had to look at my practice and ideas critically. I
have come to feel that "violent actions" have very deep-rooted
organizing effects on individual ways of relating, and that far more
intensive work is necessary to reverse such patterns, e.g. in groups
for violent men and for teenagers. I have also been influenced by the
growing concerns about the notion of the family victimization process, the traumatic effect on children (and women), and the induction of victim or perpetrator roles in turn. I have conceptualized this
as what I now describe as a "trauma-organized system". There has
been a natural link with my long-standing family therapy approach—the way that stressful and traumatic events affect the
"meaning" given to the "self" and "other". This in turn has an organizing effect on the form and patterning of family relationships
that emerge.

So having integrated my ideas with Warren Kinston in our
"Focal Family" approach for the new volume of Gurman and
Kniskern's *Handbook of Family Therapy*, it seems a good time to attempt to integrate my current ideas towards a systemic account/
view of family violence, of physical and sexual abuse, hoping that it
will make sense of what I do clinically.

The process to be followed in this book is as follows:

1. To look at "sociological perspectives" of family life, and to try to understand what makes families inherently violent institutions.
2. To describe the societal contexts that contribute to the family being a violent institution.
3. To examine the theories that account for why some families are violent to such a degree that people become hurt or damaged.
4. To introduce the issues of trauma and how traumatic events create a "traumatically organized system" and its effect on development.
5. To explain the way in which traumatically organized systems affect individual and family processes through traumagenic dynamic effects.
6. To describe the link between of trauma-organized therapy and focal family therapy—describing families and formulating a focus for work.
7. To present approaches to the investigation of trauma-organized systems—the externalizing process.
8. To present approaches to the treatment of trauma-organized systems.

At this point it is helpful to define what I mean by a *trauma-organized system*, to provide a context for the rest of this book.

Trauma-organized systems are essentially "action systems". The essential actors in the system are the victimizer who "traumatizes" and the victim who is "traumatized". By definition there is an absence of a protector, or the potential protectors are neutralized.

The victimizer is overwhelmed by impulses to actions of a physically, sexually, or emotionally abusive nature which emerge from his or her own experiences. These are felt to be overwhelming and beyond control. The cause is attributed to the "victim" who, in line with individual, familial, and cultural expectations, is construed as responsible for the victimizers feelings and intentions. Any action on the victim's part as a result of abuse, or to avoid abuse, is to be interpreted as further cause for disinhibition of violent action and justification for further abuse. Any potentially protective figure is organized or neutralized by the process of deletion and by minimization of victimizing actions or traumatic effects. Deletion and minimization characterizes the thinking processes of the victimizer and victim alike. The motto of those involved in the trauma-organized system is, "First—'see no evil'; Second—'hear no evil'; Third—'speak no evil'; and the Fourth—'think no evil'".

It is not a question of the individual creating the system, or the system creating the problem. Events in the lives of individuals create "stories" by which they live their lives, make relationships, initiate actions, respond to actions, and maintain and develop them. Abusive traumatic events have an exceptionally powerful effect in creating self-perpetuating "stories" which in turn create "trauma-organized systems" where "abusive" events are re-enacted and reinforced.

TRAUMA-ORGANIZED SYSTEMS

CHAPTER ONE

The family
as a violent institution:
a sociological perspective

THE PREVALENCE OF VIOLENCE IN THE FAMILY

S trauss and Gelles (1987) have completed a number of important sociological studies that have demonstrated the extraordinary extent of violence within the North American family—violence between men and women, parents and children, children and their peers, the widespread use of guns, objects, and so forth. Although there may be some basic differences between North America and the United Kingdom and Europe in terms of scale and particular types of violence, there are likely to be many similarities. The rate for sexual abuse, for instance, is comparable in the United Kingdom and the United States, and studies in Australia and New Zealand indicate very similar rates of child abuse as in the United Kingdom and the United States.

The theoretical position Strauss and Gelles take is not to ask *is* the family a violence-prone institution, but *how* violent, and what are the factors that make for more, rather than less, violent interactions. What makes for the extremes of family violence reported in families seen in Social Service departments and by clinicians, and how do they differ from families with similar characteristics but who are not reported to authorities? All researchers feel that families who come to note represent the tip of the iceberg.

THE FAMILY AS A VIOLENT INSTITUTION

We first need to ask how it is that the family is an institution prone to violence—rather than care. As Michael White (1989) has put it, what are the factors that prevent, or in his words *restrain*, family members from respecting each other and providing adequate care and consideration, rather than high levels of anger and rejection?

Gelles (1987) described eleven factors that made families prone to violence, rather than providing appropriate nurturance and socialization. Within these factors are issues that researchers and clinicians have observed that differentiate "abusive" from "normal" violent families (Burgess & Congar, 1978).

1. Time at risk

The ratio of time family members spend interacting with each other far exceeds the ratio of time spent interacting with others. The ratio will vary depending on stages in the family life cycle, and on cultural contexts in terms of how men, women, and children are expected to spend their time and where. The more time a family spend together, the more opportunity for conflict and violence there is. Poor environmental conditions, low income, poverty, unemployment, poor education, isolation—all are "markers" for violence in families. By *definition* such families have less space and fewer resources available to them and therefore more time at risk of conflict rather than being involved in other activities.

2. Range of activities and interests

Not only do family members generally spend a great deal of time with one another, but their interactions also range over a much wider spectrum than non-familial activities so that conflict is far more likely. There are striking differences when people are at work, compared to being in the family—e.g. sitting in an office in the company of peers, versus meeting the demands of a hungry, tem-per-tantruming toddler or a fed-up teenager.

Families where abuse occurs show a disproportionate expression of negative or aversive behaviour towards each other in the face of what may be relatively neutral differences. Abusive parents also show a tendency to perceive differences linked to ordinary development as hostile rebellious behaviour.

3. Intensity of involvement

By comparison with non-familial interaction, the quality of family interaction is also unique in terms of communication patterns, alliances, boundaries, and affects (Loader, Burck, Kinston, & Bentovim, 1981). The degree of intensity, commitment, and involvement in family interactions is, therefore, greater. A cutting remark made by a family member is likely to have a much larger impact than the same remark in another setting.

What characterizes families where abuse occurs is the presence of mutual antagonism, higher levels of criticism, threatening behaviour, more shouting—all evidence of extreme intensity of involvement. Interestingly, there is also a tendency to the reverse—an *avoidance* of interaction—perhaps as a way of *avoiding* the conflict and intensity which may feel like an inevitable script.

There is also an *absence* of desirable, warm, affectionate interaction, and coercive exchanges are maintained when they occur.

4. Impinging activities

Many interactions in the family are inherently conflict-structured with winners and losers, whether it involves deciding what television show to watch or what car to buy. Resentments are inevitable, between younger children and teenagers, boys and girls, men and women, concerning differences and choices that have to be made.

Families where abuse occurs show deficient social skills in managing these differences. Coercion is used to resolve conflicts, punishments for perceived transgressions. Such techniques are often used inconsistently and inevitably fail to achieve compliance, requiring ever-increasing power-orientated responses and aversive interchange.

5. Rights to influences

Belonging to a family implies that the most powerful member has the right to influence the values, attitudes, and behaviours of other family members. This is appropriate in social contexts where parents are expected to fulfil social obligations in relationship to children's socialization. But this may merely violate what somebody wants to do, and there is ample scope for conflict, disagreement, and resentment when a reasonable demand is made, e.g. a child wants to watch a favourite programme but is made to go to bed.

There is a continuum of parenting behaviour, the fundamental dimensions being *demandingness*—the degree of control parents attempt to exert—and *responsiveness*—the balance between interactions that are child-centred versus adult-centred. Abusive parents are either the extreme of the authoritarian—insensitive to children's level of ability and needs, using intrusive power and assertive techniques—or neglectful, insensitive, and undemanding—"anything goes". Such attitudes have a profound effect on social competence, spontaneity, formation of conscience, and intellectual performance (Maccoby & Martin, 1983).

6. Age and sex differences

The family is unique in that it is made up of different ages and sexes, with inherent societal views about gender and age and authority being enacted. There is a current high rate of reconstituted families, and in such families children and parents come together at different life stages, with different generational positions and different histories. There are major potentials for conflicts between generations, families, and sexes. Societal rules construct particular roles having more or less authority, on the basic age, sex, and generational position, regardless of the individual's capacity to fulfil them.

Families where violence occurs are characterized by patriarchal views pervading the childhood of one or both parents: women and children are accepted as appropriate victims of violence and abuse. Stresses in the current family can trigger the release of models learnt in the original family—which can be a "test bed" for violent interactions (Strauss & Kantor, 1987).

7. Ascribed roles

In addition to the problems of age and sex differences, the roles of mother and father are socially constructed. There is an assumption that a woman who has given birth could be a mother, the man who helps create a child a father; for instance, a mother of 16 and a father of 17 are expected to step into these roles. Alternatively, it is felt they could not possibly develop such a capacity.

Similarly, the man who lives with or marries a woman with a child, or a woman who marries a man with a child, becomes a stepfather, or stepmother, the children stepchildren, stepdaughters, stepsons. Thus authority and dependent relationships are defined through social construction, giving the adults rights to make demands to socialize children and expect compliance. Such demands may be inevitably conflictual, and can become abusive if there is no background of attachment, or experience of care to back up the roles taken. There is a higher rate of intra-familial violence, e.g. sexual and physical abuse, in reconstituted families. Men and women with an abusive orientation can take advantage of the roles left vacant when a parent leaves, and children may be "groomed" to become victims of abuse.

8. Privacy

The modern family is a private institution, insulated from the eyes, the ears, and often enough the rules of the wider society. Where privacy is high, social control by definition must be low. Idiosyncratic rules and family meanings can grow in isolation and can overwhelm individual differences and needs. Rules for appropriate punishment reflecting societal expectations can grow and become distorted in private. Extreme distortions of belief about appropriate punishment characterize abusive parents.

There are also distortions about children and adults as appropriate victims for punishment. The sort of violent incident to a child which would now provoke a search for a scapegoat amongst social workers, is scarcely noted if it occurs between adults. Spouse abuse, particularly abuse of women, is frequently labelled as a private domestic incident. Fortunately such attitudes are changing, but the degree of violence accepted against spouses far exceeds what is currently accepted against children. This is another aspect of the progressive social construction of what is acceptable violence and what is not.

9. Involuntary membership

There is a powerful social construction that the family is more than the individuals who make it up. The family is construed as an exclusive organization: birth relationships are the responsibility of birth parents and cannot be terminated—unless violence/breakdown patterns are such that a court deems that the degree of development impairment is too great. Politically the State construes the family as a coherent exclusive organization in an attempt to get members to take responsibility for each other rather than relying on the State. Current legal approaches to the care of children requires a high level of proof of poor care on a parent's part for the State to intervene. Indeed, current U.K. legislation prescribes that even when violence has occurred the State has to demonstrate that the alternative plan it has in mind would represent a real advantage to the child.

Whilst there can be ex-wives and ex-husbands, there can be no "ex-children" or "ex-parents"—except in extreme situations. There is a constant dialetic between State authority and the rights of children to be protected, versus children being an involuntary member of an organization—the family—whose integrity has to be protected at the expense of its members.

Being a member of a family can represent a right to expect and give care, nurturance, affection, and support. In families where abuse occurs, being a member can also involve personal, social, material, and legal commitment and entrapment. When conflict arises it is not easy to flee the scene, or resign from the group. Political responses such as not funding young people's living away from their parents increase the sense of legal entrapment.

10. Stress

Families are prone to stress. Moreover, families are constantly undergoing changes or transitions. Events of the life cycle—e.g. the birth of children, maturation of children, aging, retirement, and death—represent changes that have effects on the family group. Similarly, events that affect individuals—unemployment, illness, handicap—cause stress to be transmitted. There are also stressful events and relationship patterns that are transmitted inter-generationally, and which influence marital choice and subsequent attitudes to children (Bentovim & Kinston, 1991).

Violent means of dealing with stress is a characteristic learned response within the family context. Where abuse occurs families are characterized by being "stress-filled", and stress is dealt with by aversive rather than appropriately coping responses.

11. Extensive knowledge of social biographies

The intimacy and emotional involvement of family relationships reveals a full range of identities and roles for family members. Strengths and vulnerabilities, likes and dislikes, loves and fears are all known to family members. While this knowledge can help support a relationship, the information can also be used to attack intimates and lead to conflict. Specific attitudes and perceptions of "the other" can grow, and a deep conviction can arise about the qualities of "badness" or "goodness" of the other which is reinforced by the closed repetitive intense context of family life and character.

Thus roles of men, women, husbands, wives, boys, girls may be shaped, meanings grow and develop and roles are created and re-inforced. They are seen in their most negative forms in abusive families. The attribution of "deserving" punishment or sexual interest is the underlying matrix and gives meaning and reason for abusive action.

CHAPTER TWO

Family violence: explanatory models to describe violent and abusive families

T here are a multitude of factors that have been associated with violence in the home. Researchers have consistently found a number of factors related to various aspects of domestic violence.

The cycle of violence

The cycle of violence—the inter-generational transmission of violence—is advanced as an important factor on the basis of the following findings. The more parents are violent to children, the more violent those children are to siblings. The more violent husbands are to wives, the more violent the wife is towards her children. Violence experienced as a child, in the form of "benign" abuse, repeats a generation later. The degree of subsequent violence depends on intensity and length of victimization. Although this "trickle-down" model is generally true, it is also the case that a man who is violent to his marital partner will be disproportionately *more* violent to his children, than is the partner (Gelles, 1987).

It should be noted that these research findings are often based on "known cases", that is, those that have come to official attention. The publicly perceived strength of an association—e.g. poor social and economic situations and abuse—is often based on how *often* the finding is cited, not how *strong* the statistical association is or how well the research meets the standards of scientific evidence. Findings are initially stated with a qualification, then repeated in the literature without qualifications. Reviews cite other reviews and the strength of the finding grows without the original qualifications or evidence being confirmed through replication. In the field of family violence there are a number of explanations that have been constructed from such "empirical" findings. Explanations focus on the "individual", i.e. psychopathological; the "social context", i.e. sociocultural or ecological; or the "interactional", i.e. social-interactional.

Psychopathological explanations

Psychopathological explanations link the inability to control violent impulses towards partners or children, with that person having a pervasive sense of discontent, anger, and irritability. These basic attitudes are seen to arise from individual scars, e.g. from abuse and deprivation which affects the ability to relate. A good deal of empirical research has been carried out to test this model, but the only findings that support it indicate that abusers are more likely to be impulsive, immature, and prone to depression. Such explanations pay insufficient attention to the *processes* individuals become caught in—situational/contextual variables, ways of coping, and styles of attribution that may be more helpful in understanding which individual will abuse, where, and when.

Socio-cultural models—ecological explanations

Socio-cultural models—ecological explanations put forward the view that human behaviour should be studied in context. It is asserted that social and economic deprivation transforms predisposed high-risk individuals into abusers, and that violence is an attempt to control stressful events. Normal parents, it is argued, may be socialized into abusive practice through interactions with cultural, community, and family influences, e.g. harsh punishment in childhood, and patriarchal societal views are seen as normative. Unemployment and limited occupational opportunities are all seen as stressors that lead to abusive action.

But these factors are also not predictive of who will abuse and when, and interestingly recent research has indicated that when individuals who are abused in childhood are followed up into adulthood, they do not inevitably abuse children more frequently than other parents, although they are significantly more likely to be arrested for criminal activities. Other research indicates that there is three to five times the risk of idividuals, abused in childhood, abusing their own child, compared to those who have not been abused (Straus & Kantor, 1987).

But one immediately has to ask what the factors are that protect those individuals who, reversing their own abusive experience, develop a more positive attitude to children. Other research that has followed vulnerable individuals into adulthood has indicated that positive parenting is to do with availability of some positive relationship during childhood, which may include a psychotherapeutic experience (Egeland, 1988).

Social-interactional explanations

Social-interactional explanations focus on the interactional processes between parent and child within the specific familial context, in the context of larger social structures, to explain why some parents abuse.

Some of the findings from this approach have already been referred to (chapter one). Research findings do support some interactional differences in families where abuse occurs compared to non-abusive families of similar social backgrounds. The important differences are the presence of reciprocation of aversive behaviour, reinforcement of inappropriate behaviour, ineffective use of punishment, negative emotional response, and arousal towards children. Stable, global negative attributions exist about children and partners who are subsequently victimized, which predispose to grievance and anger. Such explanations involve a dynamic interplay among the individual, the family, and society, and these processes will be described in some detail later. It can be stated with some confidence that violence—whether physical, sexual, or emotional—is the result of an interaction within a system that seldom provides alternative solutions or restraints. Recent developments are demonstrating that such violent experiences are registered in the developing brain—the "mirror" of development.

CHAPTER THREE

Developing
a social-interactional–systemic
account of family violence

A lthough, as we have seen in chapter one, the social organization of the family by definition makes it prone to conflict, the social-interactional approach argues that the family must be seen within a cultural context where violence is tolerated, accepted, and even mandated for. Dobash and Dobash (1979), two of the strongest proponents of a feminist gender-based view of family violence, describe women in society as "appropriate victims" of family violence and seen as deserving of blame and punishment. Generally physical punishment in the bringing up of children is still widely accepted. Although attempts in Scandinavia to construct a view that children should not be hit has shown some evidence of success, there is a broadly accepted view that within families it is permissible, or even proper, to hit people you love, for more powerful people to hit less powerful people, and to use hitting to achieve some end or goal.

Although the argument about the use of violence appears to refer to physical violence, the same argument in my view extends to sexual or emotional violence. In this context sexual violence is an act perpetrated not as a mutual act freely enjoyed by partners who can consent, but as an act initiated for the satisfaction of one

13

individual without the consent of a partner, or with a partner who by reason of age or understanding could not give consent.

Thus there is an implicit view in society that sex can occur without consent, that the more powerful people can demand sexual favours from the less powerful, and that sexuality may be used to achieve ends or goals such as power or control. Equally, emotional abuse, denigration, disqualification, criticism, hostility may each similarly be used with those who are loved, with the less powerful, and to achieve ends or goals.

It is only truly possible to understand the phenomenon of violence within family contexts, whether physical, sexual or emotional, by taking an approach that attempts to involve society, the individual, and the family.

We (Kinston, 1987; Bentovim & Kinston, 1991) showed that the social-interactional approach comprises the *individual*, the *family*, and *society* as key elements, each of which in turn is a system. The experiences that define society, families, and individuals are distinct but dependent on each other (see Figure 1). Societies' experiences are defined in terms of attitudes, norms, rights, and values. These persist largely through the family, which serves as the agent that transmits and reproduces culture. The family depends on the societal context for support and legitimization and for its own sense of value. The family's experiences are defined in terms of its own interactions and meanings, and it is itself reproduced by individuals in the family, since individuals are nurtured and socialized by the family.

At the same time individuals create and regulate interactions and meanings within the family. The circle is completed as individuals conform or react to (or, all too rarely, transform) society. At the same time, society recognizes and assigns values to individuals through their activities and achievements. Inevitably, despite claims to the contrary, as family therapists we have until recently largely ignored society and have concerned ourselves with interaction between the family and individual members, with varying degree of emphasis on the family as a whole, or on the individual member, or on the interaction between the two. Family therapists are now thinking far more about social justice and the relationship between family therapists and other systems.

We cannot ignore society and societal values when we think of violence. Figure 2 shows the relationship between the individual, the family, and the cultural setting which initiates and maintains violent interactions. Violence is placed in the centre to emphasize that it does not uniquely belong to any single setting, but can be seen as a property of each. Society is thus seen as containing attitudes, norms, rights, and values about "appropriate" violence—what is permitted against whom and in what circumstances. The family contains violence for the setting of the violent act. Society legitimizes violence and sees the violence or "discipline" of family members as being approved in its proper place and sanctions sexual activities and expectations. Violent interactions and roles are an integral aspect of this process and in turn create and regulate such meanings within the family and feed back to contain them. Society contains individuals who conform to or react against attitudes concerning violence and violent behaviour, whether physical, sexual, or emotional.

Weakness, vulnerability, and dependency are central unifying and common features of all types of family violence, and until recently there has been an extraordinary lack of social consequences for aggression of all types within the family. Sociological investigators conclude that the benefits of aggression, even including the injury to the victim, often outweigh the cost. The history of recognition of different forms of family violence attest to this. There is a far higher profile of concern about abused children in the media since the Maria Colwell case in the 1970s, and far lower for the often horrendous physical violence and injury seen in wife battering. Indeed, it is only recently that the crime of rape in marriage has been recognized.

Society constructs a different value and view of a man who attacks his wife for what he perceives as justifiable slights, compared to views about women who retaliate, who may be blamed more. The woman who cannot escape from the violent home, and cannot protect her child, is often more powerfully condemned than the man who perpetrates the violence itself. Only recently has there been some understanding for the women whose only escape is to kill the man who abused her.

16

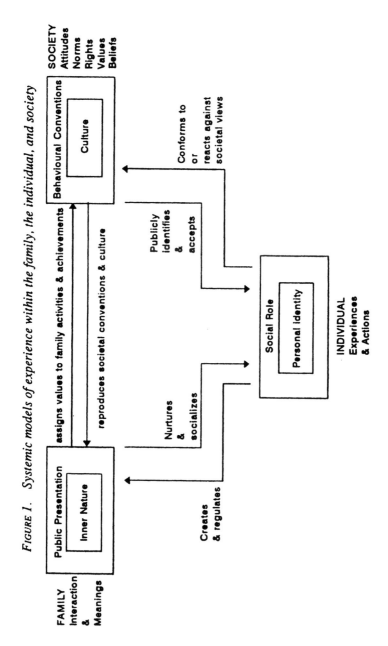

FIGURE 1. *Systemic models of experience within the family, the individual, and society*

FIGURE 2. Relationships between the individual, the family, and society and violence

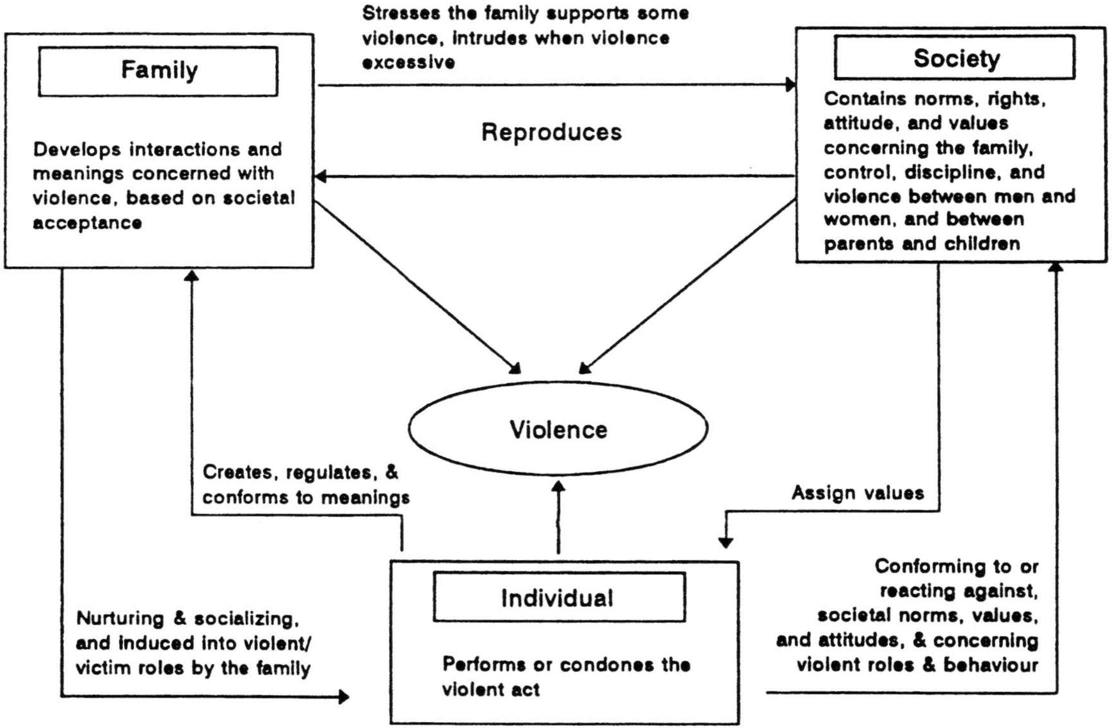

Society

Contains norms, rights, attitude, and values concerning the family, control, discipline, and violence between men and women, and between parents and children

Stresses the family supports some violence, intrudes when violence excessive

Reproduces

Family

Develops interactions and meanings concerned with violence, based on societal acceptance

Assign values

Conforming to or reacting against, societal norms, values, and attitudes, & concerning violent roles & behaviour

Violence

Individual

Performs or condones the violent act

Creates, regulates, & conforms to meanings

Nurturing & socializing, and induced into violent/victim roles by the family

17

THE SOCIAL CONSTRUCTION
OF FAMILY VIOLENCE

Although we are now familiar with notions of child abuse or of domestic spouse abuse, it is important to recall that these terms are relatively recent in use. The definitions expand and change as new forms of abuse are described—e.g. the recent concern with ritual abuse. There is a constant process of social definition, construction, de-construction, and reconstruction of these concepts. Therefore the boundaries of family violence contract or expand with changing societal belief systems. In my view there are sufficient similarities between physical, sexual, and emotional abuse to see them as different facets of family violence.

We tend to define different forms of abuse as those cases which come to professional and official attention, or those individuals who choose to seek professional help or flee to a shelter. Thus there is often confusion between the factors that lead people to come forward and therefore to be publicly labelled as victims or as abusers, and the factors that actually cause men to abuse women, parents to abuse children, and lead to the perpetration of other forms of family violence.

SELF-FULFILLING PROPHECIES
AND FAMILY VIOLENCE

These labelling processes become self-fulfilling and built into the system. Family violence is more often associated with certain structural issues such as social class, culture, and values. We ourselves saw, in setting up a treatment programme, that families in contact with social agencies, and therefore more under scrutiny, were more likely to reveal evidence of abuse and be referred for treatment. People in higher social classes have many more mechanisms for maintaining a distance from social control agencies and use other agencies—such as the law, medicine, the media—to challenge the label and the diagnosis. Yet surveys of adults describing their abusive experiences in childhood indicate a broad spectrum of social class backgrounds. Indeed, recent research indicates that the previously socially constructed view of the "weakness" of women, due to a higher incidence of emotional or phobic disorders in adult life, may well be brought about by their greater vulnerability to abuse, both in childhood and in adult life (Mullen et al., 1988).

An example of this process was revealed during therapeutic work with Ann C, a teacher in her early 40s who came originally with her husband, a lawyer, for marital work following his discovery of an affair she had with a fellow teacher. She was absolutely torn in her affections between her husband and her lover. She felt the need for security with her husband and children, although their sexual life had failed for some years. Yet she was far more excited by the relationship with her colleague and experienced intense sadistic and masochistic fantasies about him. It seemed impossible for her to construct a whole relationship, with "parenting" and "sexuality" in the one relationship. In an individual session that she requested, she revealed that her relationship history had been "wild" and promiscuous before she settled down to "parenting" without "sexuality" with her husband. She had lived with her mother and stepfather after her parents separated, and she described her stepfather's intense interest in her during her early adolescence. This involved watching her in the bathroom, touching her, and stroking her. She experienced confusion over his secret excitement and over the feeling of power she had over him, and guilt re her mother.

She connected this with her wild "secret" perverse sexuality, contrasted with the "safety" of the asexual relationship with the man she had chosen to marry and have children with. She saw this linking to her picture of her "safe" but distant father, contrasted with the excitement and perversity of her stepfather.

It was only some years later that she began to perceive her stepfather's behaviour as perverse, intrusive, and abusive. She realized she had maintained the secrecy out of a fear that her mother's second marriage would break down, and that her guilt and feelings of responsibility for her stepfather's interest in her was totally misplaced—that he had "brought forward" her confused and perverse sexual feelings and had deeply affected her capacity to make a "whole" relationship.

We will later see this pattern as an example of the long-term traumagenic dynamic effects of abuse on her self-perception, views about sexual relationships, and relationships with men and parenting. There were widespread effects on her life, and she saw herself as having a number of unconnected selves (multiple-personality formulation).

THE EFFECT OF RECOGNIZING ABUSE

One important effect of the "discovery" and the social construction of child abuse has been some evidence of a real drop in incidence recently. Re-examining families in 1985 in the way they had in 1975, Strauss and Gelles (1987) showed a decline of 40% in the rates of violence to children, as reported by a random sample of parents contacted. This meant that in North America, one in twenty-five children between 3 and 17 years of age was a victim of very severe violence in 1975, as against one in thirty-three children in 1985. During the same period there was a striking increase in numbers reported to agencies each year. Their explanation was that the change could have come about by media coverage influencing attitudes and an increased awareness of the need to report abuse. A fear of disclosure could also lead to a change in behaviour. If parents' consciousness was raised about the inappropriateness of violence, then the process of reducing violence towards children began.

VIOLENCE OF MEN TOWARDS WOMEN
AND OF WOMEN TOWARDS MEN

The same research group indicated that there had also been a drop in violence of men towards women over the same period. A debate has arisen as to whether domestic violence should be described as a general—i.e. "humanist"—issue to be owned by men and women or as a "gender" issue because of the preponderance of male partner abuse. McNeely and Mann (1990) stated that "the socially constructed" ownership of domestic violence by a single gender group ultimately serves to fragment the array of resources needed to address the problem successfully. They put forward a view that "recognition that women perpetrate domestic violence just as men do would heighten awareness of the pervasiveness of this cultures' recourse to violence".

Bograd's (1990) response is that large-scale survey data loses distinctions in the analysis, and she feels that gender differences do emerge when incidents of domestic violence are put back into the particular situational and social context in which they occurred. She suggests that men may use extreme violence to control and dominate, whilst women use lethal violence in order to escape. Acts that are similar in form may not be equivalent in meaning or consequence for husbands and wives, or people generally. She asks whether violence is sanctioned for wives as it is for husbands. Does self-protection mean the same thing to wives and to husbands? Does the woman's perception of her role as mother or wife constrain or promote her use of violence? Out of this, Bograd puts forward the view that two perspectives, feminist or humanist, create a false dichotomy and that we need "to simultaneously describe violence as a human issue and as a gender issue".

CHAPTER FOUR

Family victimization processes and social-interaction explanations for family violence

W hat are the characteristics of family violence—of sexual abuse, physical abuse, and emotional abuse? What are the processes involved when victimization occurs within a family context? *Victimization* in various forms of abuse can take the form of terrorizing, spurning, isolating, corrupting, and denying responsiveness (emotional abuse and neglect), hitting, beating, punching, burning, and stifling (physical abuse), sexual fondling and penetrative attempts (sexual abuse), poisoning and illness induction (Munchausen-by-proxy, illness-inducing syndrome).

By definition, family members subjected to such victimization, disorganization, and coercion will suffer traumatic stress effects. *Stress* is defined as a "disequilibratory event which temporarily disturbs functioning and initiates a chain of adaptive or maladaptive responses". *Traumatic stress* represents stressful events of such magnitude that the effects are overwhelming.

I find it helpful to see *victimizing actions* and *traumatic effects* as the elements of the trauma-organized system, bringing together the traumatizing effects with the notion of an organized system.

ORGANIZED SYSTEMS

Anderson, Goolishian, and Windermans (1986) introduced the notion of *problem*-determined or *problem*-organized systems. They defined these as "social action systems" defined by those actively involved in communication about a particular problem. They based their thinking on constructivist views, concerning the way communication *about* problems creates a system—a problem-determined, or problem-organized, system. The way of communicating in turn becomes the problem. Helping the problem-determined or problem-organized system to find a new way of communicating and talking and thinking about itself becomes a therapeutic aim.

I see a parallel in the way that the highly traumatic events, interactions, and responses to family violence come to "organize" the reality and perceptions of those participating—including the professionals involved. This then in turn becomes the problem system to be resolved. Furniss (1983) described the way that professionals "by proxy" reflected the perceptions and interactions of abusive family members. Thus the responsibility of the abuser is minimized, the mother or child is blamed, and the protection needs of the child and mother are ignored, rather than responsibility being placed where it belongs.

THE EFFECTS OF TRAUMA

Trauma comes from the Greek word meaning "to pierce". In the context of physical injury it implies that "skin is broken", that something intact has been breached. It implies a certain intensity of violence, with long-standing consequences for the organism.

From the physical notion of trauma the notion of psychological trauma arises: an event that in a similar intense or violent way ruptures the protective layer surrounding the mind with equally long-lasting consequences for psychic well-being. Helplessness overwhelms, mastery is undermined, defences fail, there is a sense of failure of protection, disintegration, acute mental pain as the memory of the event intrudes and replays itself repeatedly. The traumatic stress response thus imperceptibly becomes the "posttraumatic state".

"Coping with the uncopable" takes a number of forms. The form of the "post-traumatic stress state" (Eth & Pynoss, 1985) depends on the nature of the abuse. The basic response is the replaying and re-enactment of the event thrust into experience, e.g. through flash-backs triggered by reminders, spontaneously, or during play, through dreams or nightmares. There are struggles to overcome these experiences by "avoidance" or attempts to delete reminders, avoiding places, people, situations that trigger memories; or through dissociation—a form of "self-hypnotism" which blanks the experience out, creating a hole in the mind. Finally the overwhelm-ing traumatic experience can induce a state of arousal, irritability, and can effect sleep and the ability to relax.

THE EFFECTS OF
LONGER-TERM VICTIMIZATION
AND TRAUMA

Traumatic stresses in family violence—whether physical, sexual, or emotional—are characteristically not one-off events, but are re-peated and accumulate over time. They are frequently associated with secretiveness, minimization, threats, and denial as part of the victimization process.

Repeated traumatic stress is associated with extreme emotional responses, e.g. serious depressive and suicidal reactions. There can be a major dissociation, leading to multiple-personality formation. Terr (1991) has described the numbing, deep sense of outrage, and a sense of futurelessness that occurs in multiple-traumatic events. Some sort of sense has to be made of such uncontrolled stress in a necessary search for meaning, a search for what is meaningless to the person experiencing it.

Seligman (1975) and Stratton and Swaffer (1988) have described the way that stressful uncontrollable events may be attributed to the self. "I must have done something to make my father so angry with me, to hit me, humiliate me, or to abuse me sexually." This leads in turn to a sense of guilt, and a poor sense of self-worth. A stable, universal, and pervasive attribution or belief may arise that harsh punitive abusive treatment at home is representative of the way the world treats children. Social responses from peers are perceived as hostile; an affectionate response is perceived as a sexual invitation or attack.

Such responses have been described as "traumagenic dynamics" by Finklehor (1987) and represent the way traumatic events are processed and reality is personally constructed. They include the core dynamics of *powerlessness* associated with the feeling of invasion and physical pain of sexual-physical abuse, the absence of protection in the environment, and the repeated sense of helplessness associated with the victimization process of whatever nature. Figure 3 illustrates the way such effects can create their own systemic response for the individual, with helplessness, compliance, and power-orientated responses alternating. Such responses interact with and are reinforced in the familial and social context (see chapter three).

Feelings of *stigmatization* are linked to the contempt, blaming, and denigration so often associated with all forms of abuse, and are associated with self-blaming and poor self-image. *Betrayal* is felt through the manipulation of trust, violation of care, and lack of protection in the family, again a part of most victimizing patterns. This is associated with clinging and suspiciousness. *Sexualization* is the premature and distressing arousing of sexual response in sexual abuse through inappropriate responses being rewarded, or through induction to a sexual partner role or to violent sexual roles.

Traumagenic dynamics effects can have long-term organizing effects on personality and on attributional and relationship styles. They form the matrix for a powerful "story" for the self and other, through enactments and re-enactments of the original experience. Through processes of "inter-locking" pathology, traumagenic dynamics effects can influence the choice of partner, parenting styles, and ways of relating to children.

These processes are illustrated in the cases presented below.

Lorraine

This case is an example of the effects of the victimizing process and induction of a severe traumatic state.

Lorraine had been horrendously sexually and physically abused by her father and mother over some years. The abuse had gradually

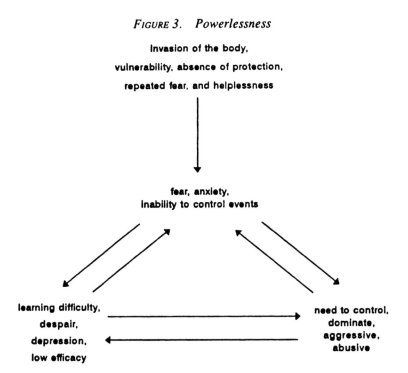

FIGURE 3.   Powerlessness

come to light; she had first described physical abuse to her teacher at school, but no evidence was found and she was branded a liar. It was only later that she was able to describe sexual abuse, for which there was ample evidence. She was interviewed at the age of 13, sitting, clinging to her social worker's lap. The therapist asked: "Was Lorraine ever angry with her father and mother?" She did not reply, and he addressed the same question to the worker. She said that sometimes Lorraine does become angry with her parents, particularly when she realizes they have totally rejected her, have completely denied the abuse, for which they had been committed to prison whilst awaiting trial. At other times, the worker indicated, Lorraine becomes sad, unhappy, and misses her parents; then she does not blame them.

Lorraine then joined in the conversation and said that if her mother had realized she was doing wrong she would *not* have gone on doing it. She did not think that either of her parents were to blame, because they could not help it, they did not know what they were doing. If they did know they would have stopped. The therapist then wondered who was responsible, was she?—Lorraine clung to her worker—the therapist said he did not think so. How could a girl of 8, or a child of any age, want an adult or both her parents to do physically violent or sexual things to her, hurt her, abuse her?

He asked that if Lorraine had seen a story in a newspaper of a girl of her age who had a rope put around her neck, was made unconscious by tightening it, and had woken up to find herself being abused, whether she would then have been angry, or would also feel that those grown-ups could not help it—particularly if they had threatened to kill her if she spoke. Lorraine clung closer and could not respond; she appeared to be in a dissociative state.

The therapist thought that if Lorraine constructed a picture of her mother and father as bad and hurtful, then she would feel she had no mother and father at all. Thus it would be better to construct a story that saw them as not being to blame, not able to help it. Then she could hold on to her parents. Lorraine relaxed.

Lorraine appeared to construct a reality where she was powerless, betrayed, stigmatized, could not allow herself to be angry, often felt she was in the wrong. She dissociated and spent many hours not thinking, living in a "hole" literally, and holding on to her parents through a total distortion of herself and the issue of their responsibilities. This was an example of being in a severely traumatized state, with her life being organized by traumagenic dynamics effects of her lengthy abuse.

In the following period she had major difficulties in making sense of the contact others made with her. She often felt abused by what was ordinary closeness. Contact set off flash-backs and intense memories, and she was unsure whether it was a memory or an actual experience. At times she felt that she should use desperate means—to prostitute herself—to regain her mother's caring, and she began to transform the abusive memories by sexualizing and eroticizing them. However, at other times she could be assertive, angry, and self-caring.

Carmel

This is an example of the way in which early victimization by a sibling organized ways of seeing herself and relating, and the way subsequent serious battering by a partner is processed and justified.

Carmel's half sibling abused her sexually from the age of 11 years. She described the way she learnt to comply; he would groom her, give her presents. She felt that it was worth trying to please him, as it gave her privileges. Her mother's only comment when she eventually told her was the contemptuous response that it was a waste to give herself to him—her half brother. She later continued a career and the story of trying to please her partners. She followed them to various parts of the world, left her children to be with them, putting the needs to comply and please her male partner before her children. She changed her name and her children's name for her current partner, accepted that he had a wife and a child the same age as the baby he had with her, and that he shared his time off from work between both families.

When her partner discovered she had been talking with an old boyfriend whom she had sought out to fill her loneliness, he became consumed with grievance, with fear of loss. He was determined to "find the truth—which he knew already". He bound her with tape, beat her, and abused her anally then said to the police, when she managed to escape, that it was sexual bondage, not abuse. She felt later, however, that his anger with her was justified. Her life was basically bad—her powerless, betrayed, and stigmatized roles. In addition she had prostituted herself previously. But she felt that he should not have been the executioner.

She could paint a convincing picture of a magical reality with him, which, although she knew that it was false, was the redeeming narrative she held on to. Whatever he did she would do anything to hold him and defied the rest of the world, who wanted to protect her.

Carl J

This case illustrates the way that an early violent, punitive, abusive upbringing organized the way of perceiving one's self and others. Carl J's response was to adopt an abusive role and organize a traumatic system extending to his family, the professional context, and the courts.

Carl J, aged 36, told a story of serious physical abuse in childhood, a father who was punitive and controlling, and a mother who was distant and uninvolved. He was a man of considerable intelligence who construed an active controlling role and story to his life. He became a helicopter pilot and was captivated by flying, by speed, by activity. When seen he had not been working for some time because of a "long-standing back problem". This did not stop him flying for pleasure, but it did prevent him from working, he said. He demanded absolute compliance in relationships. He had two children, boys, from his marriage and had abused his wife's daughter from her first marriage. His stepdaughter was terrified of him and lived in a foster home, because her mother was pulled between her desire to believe her daughter, and her compliant sharing of Carl's story that there had been no abuse. In a session when she began to articulate this conflict for herself, Carl reminded her that she had said that she could only believe her daughter's abuse story if she had seen it with her own eyes.

Carl's stepdaughter's inability to testify in the criminal trial, even through a video-link, then convinced him that he could claim that he had not abused her. He terrified and bullied workers who attempted to talk to him about the problems of him having access to his own sons. He believed he could control the court and could write his own conditions without respect or regard to anyone else.

In a session to assess relationships with his sons, his 4-year-old, who was behaving in a bullying and aggressive manner in the nursery group, began to demonstrate how "identification with the aggressor" was initiated. He echoed every statement of his father's, mimicked him, and aggressively banged on the table; one could see the terrifying, self-created image that his father lived out being adopted by his son. His father was the god who must have everything and be everything, whilst others could only comply and accept his reality.

CHAPTER FIVE

A systematic account of the different trauma-organized systems in various forms of family violence

E mpirical research and clinical observation are now beginning to present a more systematic account of the elements that make up trauma-organized systems in various family violence patterns. A key element is the attachment pattern between parent and child.

ATTACHMENT PATTERNS AND PHYSICAL AND EMOTIONAL ABUSE AND NEGLECT

Physical and emotional abuse and neglect represent extreme abnormalities of parenting. Therefore a major deficiency of attachment behaviour occurs between parents and children, and such patterns are an integral component of the trauma-organized system.

There is a great deal of confirmatory evidence that attachment patterns between parents and children where abuse occurs are highly insecure (Egeland & Sroufe, 1981; Crittenden, 1988). Empirical investigations with adults who were abused as children are now defining the way that these patterns originate and develop and their specific effects on relationship patterns. To explore these patterns it is first necessary to describe normative patterns of attachment.

Normative patterns of attachment

When parents and infants show *normative* patterns of attachment, investigation reveals parents who have a good recall of their childhood. They give a coherent account of traumatic and stressful experiences and appear to have "worked through" and learnt from them. They are responsive, sensitive parents, and their toddlers are secure, show appropriate distress on separations, but are positive when reunited and loving. In pre-school such children are self-reliant and socially competent, neither victim nor exploiter. They are perceived as likeable and are expected to be age-appropriate once they get to school. They develop models that are open to new information and revision (Crittenden, 1988). These are important observations because they imply that stress and traumatic events do not *have* to organize future realities, and children of abused parents are not fated to repeat history.

Insecure patterns of attachment

Insecure patterns of attachment are described as (1) *avoidant*, encompassing the rejecting nature of the relationship; (2) *re-enacting* or *reversing*, encompassing the nature and form of the relationship; or (3) *disorganized*, referring to the disruptive effect of the relationship.

Avoidant patterns

Avoidant attachment patterns in families are characterized by parents who are *rejecting* in their response to their infants, aversive and wooden in their contact with them. Their infants are *avoidant* of contact when attempts are made to pick them up and play with them. Minimal emotional responses are shown following separation; the infants avoid contact on reunion and remain guarded. They seem to have developed what we described as a "shell" of apparent indifference and self-sufficiency (Bentovim & Kinston,

1991) which persists. Being treated as a thing, the "world" in turn is treated as a thing and as of no importance; models are created that are "closed" to new information, and such patterns can persist through childhood into adult life (Crittenden, 1988).

When adults who show avoidant responses, or appear to have been subjected to similar parenting, are asked about their childhood they idealize their experiences. They deny and dismiss early hurts and have poor recall for them. This is similar to what we described as "deletion" patterns when referring to stressful and traumatic events (Bentovim & Kinston, 1991).

Re-enacting or reversing patterns

The second type of insecure attachment is more "active" in form: anger, neglect, coercion, clinging, or rejection are the characteristic behavioural patterns observed.

Parents are observed to be either *intrusive* with their infants or *rejecting* towards them. Infants are intensely *ambivalent* on separation and can be *angry* on reunion or *cling*.

Children who earlier showed an inconsistent mixture of anger and neglect respond with coercive behaviour to others in pre-school settings. They may be sullen and oppositional, and their "closed" model of the world—in which are perceived constant threats and hostility—is countered by the use of power-orientated responses. They are later perceived as aggressive, miserable children showing conduct difficulties, taking their identity by re-enacting their aggressive experiences (George & Main, 1979).

Children shown consistent anger or neglect develop a "defensive" shell; alternatively, they may cling and display *compliant* roles in relationships with other adults and children to gain attention. Thus they identify with the victim role.

Parents who perpetuate angry or neglectful patterns of parenting reveal that they remain enmeshed in and preoccupied with the past. They are full of anger and resentment and are seen to be re-enacting or re-experiencing their traumatic or stressful experiences in relation to their children.

To such parents, normal children's behaviour is perceived, interpreted, and attributed as being intrinsically negative and out of control—abusive—and creates a feeling of threat for the parent.

Punishment is justified to gain some measure of control; there is an increased perception of the child as being bad and deserving further punishment. Rejection and negative interaction patterns become reflexive and can relieve the parents' tension, and may even feel momentarily invigorating. There can be a reversal of roles, the abused, abuser.

Disorganized patterns

The third pattern is the recently described "disorganized" pattern of attachment. This is characterized by confusion, distress, fluctuating anger, and misery. Parents seem to be living out their own unresolved stressful and traumatic experiences to an even greater degree. Typically, traumatic-stress or loss responses predominate. Instead of anger and resentment—which could be seen as a structured, organized form of "survival" through "reversing" abusive contexts—traumatic-confusion reactions continue and children cling or are dazed, distressed.

Avoiding the development of abusive patterns
in parents who have themselves been abused

It has already been indicated that there is a three to five times risk of people who have been abused in childhood co-creating, as it were, their own childhood through interactions with their children. The question is, what about parents who do not re-enact their past abuse?

Egeland (1988) carried out an important long-term follow-up of the parenting styles of women who had been abused in their own childhood. He found that such parents are less likely to abuse if they themselves had *one* individual in their own lives with whom they had a positive relationship, whether this person came from within or outside the family. It was interesting to note that one of these positive influences was an experience of being in psychotherapy during their own childhood or adolescence. It would seem, therefore, that having a redeeming relationship can give a model that counteracts abusive organizing constructions.

These observations confirm the importance of interventions to ensure that children who are abused and neglected have some positive experiences in their life to countermand their abusive realities. Such experiences can initiate a different cycle of relating which can reverse rather than maintain aversive responses, and initiate more positive responses to their partners and children.

THE TRAUMA-ORGANIZED SYSTEM
OF PHYSICAL ABUSE

To illustrate the trauma-organized system of physical abuse, an interview with parents and their young child is described. The therapist's role is eliciting the processes, through a knowledge of characteristic feelings and responses of parents who abuse physically.

Jamie was 3 years old at the time of the interview to be reported. Cathy and Richard, the parents, had been seen previously when Jamie was 3 months, following a leg injury. At that time it was not possible to establish who had abused Jamie, but it was assumed to be the father as he showed violent responses to Cathy. Eventually the parents separated and Jamie was reunited with his mother in a residential unit. She had done some work on what had been a long-standing difficult relationship with her own mother. Just before we saw them again, the parents indicated that they wanted to get back together. Cathy revealed that *she* had abused Jamie, and that the allegations against Richard of violence were in fact a distraction to cover up the reality of her abuse of Jamie, which she could not face. The interview had the aim of establishing whether some further work was possible to create a safe context for Jamie with his two parents living together.

Therapist: Can you tell me what happened?

Cathy: I felt everything would be easy when Jamie was first born—I was 18 at the time. But when he was born, I found I got very tired. I couldn't relax with him at night. I had to lie awake

Here Cathy is describing the increasing sense of stress, grievance, depression, and conflict. She describes her growing anger, and the therapist assumes she is blaming the child for keeping her awake.

waiting for his crying, having
to get up, getting really tired
and depressed. I didn't know
what I really wanted. I
wanted Jamie, but I wanted
my own life as well.
Tiredness was one of the
main things. It must have
caused the way I reacted—
looking back. I didn't want
him to wake up, I'd lay
awake waiting—I would
wake up and it would drive
me absolutely insane—it's
hard to explain. It made me
snap at him—through the
crying. I couldn't cope with
crying.

Therapist: It sounds as though
you were developing a
grievance about him—even
though you probably
thought this was stupid.
Perhaps you saw him not as
Jamie, but as a crying,
screaming monster, making
it hard to control yourself.

The therapist is tracking, naming the process, framing it as understandable response.

Cathy: Yes, that's right—it was
as if I could flip at any
second—then with the
broken leg.

Therapist: What was the
process that led to the leg
injury?

Cathy: I was so tired, he was
with a friend to give me a
break. But I still couldn't

Cathy describes increasing resentment and blaming; that he slept with someone else. She sleep. I was so worried about him. Immediately I heard he'd slept through the night with her—that got to me. I used to sit pushing the pram backwards and forwards—getting more and more tired. Immediately he came to me he started crying again.

then describes the immediate aversive or disorganized attachment response with herself.

Cathy: I gave him feeds, he kept on screaming. I flipped. I seemed to be thinking very quickly. I grabbed him. His little legs were kicking. I grabbed them; I didn't realize what I had done—I shouldn't have done it. I went from up there (emotionally) to down there. From being so up-tight to cuddling him. It had got to the stage when he began to dominate me.

Here Cathy is describing the "reflexive" angry response, relieving her tensions and then releasing her sympathy—by cuddling him. She alludes to the reversal, the sense of baby being seen as the dominating parent, and she as the victimized child she had felt in her own childhood.

Therapist (after commenting on the distress of loving and hating someone so): What stopped you sharing this with Richard?

Richard (interjecting): Perhaps it was the place we were living in (one room only).

Richard is referring to the multiple stresses, limited accommodation, and their fears of loss.

Therapist: What did you think she'd do?

Richard: Do the same to her.

Cathy: I thought he'd leave me,

It was interesting to note, even at this point, that Jamie played closer to his father and engaged him in activities. When Cathy was asked to give him a "cuddle" he squirmed away and the hate me for it—the pressure of one room. I blamed him.

longer-term aversive pattern was still evident.

It was possible, however, with responsibility for the abuse having been taken, to explore the origins of the negative interactions and to formulate a treatment plan to change the trauma-organized system. This involved the family living in a residential unit, with therapeutic work aimed at improving the parents' relationship and helping them sort out the connections with their own experiences of being parented and the way this in turn connected with their relationship and parenting in turn. Specific parent–child work would be essential to test whether abusive interactions could be replaced by caring ones.

Clinical example of physical and emotional abuse

Dennis H is a second case of physical and emotional abuse, but at a later stage, without adequate treatment. Dennis was referred at age 13 with conduct problems and poor growth. He was described by his boarding school as one of the most difficult boys in the school—sly, devious, digging and poking other children in an aggressive way, rebellious, and defiant. His eating habits were very variable: he would either eat enormous amounts or reject everything. There was a long history of concern about both Dennis and his younger sister, Jean, because of neglect and physical abuse of Dennis.

Jean was very much the favourite of her mother, and there were concerns that there was some sexualized contact with her by her mother. The father was laid back in the extreme. He would never take any positive action to intervene in his wife's harsh discipline of Dennis. There was a long history of marital conflict, and he appeared to take a strongly conflict-avoiding stance. Mrs H herself felt she had the whole burden of control of the children, acknowledged her own harsh up-bringing, and wanted to reverse this with her own children, but found that Dennis' behaviour "set her going". She described an episode in a joint meeting with Dennis. He made what he felt to be an ordinary request to see a particular television programme. She perceived this as his defiance. This had triggered her rage. She described herself hitting him with a belt and leaving weals.

Dennis described his continuing fear of his mother—to her surprise—and also his sense of grievance and outrage. This provoked his distrust and aggressive style in school, which then provoked further blaming and punishment by his mother for his failure to behave well. In turn this was reinforced by the "over-positive" relationship between the mother and Jean, and was maintained by the separateness between the parents and the father's absence from the scene through "work" and non-intervention.

Not surprisingly the emotional atmosphere affected Dennis' ability to eat and to grow, and he also showed signs of emotional dwarfism. Following this sharing of Dennis' long-standing fear and sense of powerlessness, hidden by aggression, and the mother's despair at her attempts to reverse her own harsh parenting, mother and son went out to eat. He ate a pizza, and half of her's.

This case demonstrates the long-standing nature of the trauma-organized system of physical and emotional abuse, the effect on the key players, and the way the family context is created and maintains it.

THE TRAUMA-ORGANIZED SYSTEM
OF SEXUAL ABUSE

The trauma-organized system of sexual abuse consists of the victimizing action on the part of the abuser. "Sexualization" is the traumatic response characteristic of the individual who is not giving consent or cannot give consent.

Sexual victimizing processes

A review of what is known about the "victimizing processes" involved in sexual abuse (Bentovim & Davenport, 1992) includes two major factors which underlie the behaviours and action of the perpetrator. These are (1) the substitution of sexual responses for normal affectionate contacts, the "sexualization of inter-personal relationships", and (2) the use of sexual victimizing responses to assert power and control over the other, the "sexualization of subordination".

It is important to note that whereas physical abuse and neglect is perpetuated by men and women, men and boys are responsible for

95% of child sexual abuse. A significant number of such individuals have themselves been sexually or physically abused, and an examination of the effects of abuse in the long term on boys may help understand the origin of victimizing behaviour.

The *traumatic sexualization characteristic* of sexual abuse and the *powerlessness* of sexual, physical, and emotional abuse have profound effects on the identity and meaning system of the individual. There are major differences in the way abusive activities are processed by boys and girls. Flash-backs and memories of abusive acts may be responded to actively by boys, through identification with the abuser, leading to sexualizing and abusing others. Girls more commonly respond in a more "victim" mode. To observe this a clinical example is given (see Figure 4)

Darren, aged 15, described prolonged confusing flash-backs, both of his own abuse and of the sexual activities he was forced to enact with his sister. He could literally feel the image of his father taking him over, and he realized that it was through this identification that he began the process of thinking sexually about children he knew, masturbating to the thoughts. He then felt impelled to find and seek out children. He knew that if he persuaded a child to allow him to abuse them, whether with threats or bribes, he would feel some satisfaction and release even though he would then feel guilty, ashamed, distressed. But the cycle of flash-backs of his own abuse and his ways of coping would take over and be developed into a reflexive "abusive cycle", which he felt controlled him rather than him controlling it, and which developed its own momentum.

The trauma-organizing dynamic of *powerlessness* acts in boys like Darren by stimulating an aggressive dominating response. This goes hand-in-hand with the sexualization response to find someone who literally can take over their own traumatized self-representation, someone who reminds them of their powerlessness and can be made to feel it instead. Finding emotional *closeness* through sexuality to compensate for rejecting is another commonly reported experience. Focusing on someone younger and less powerful acts as a source of sexual satisfaction, assertion of power, and emotional closeness. The sense of powerlessness—sexual, emotional, and physical—is briefly but addictively overcome and bears the seeds of repetition and re-enaction.

FIGURE 4.   Traumatic sexualization

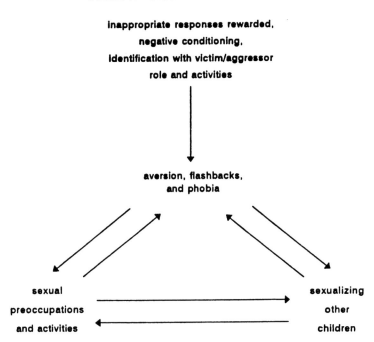

Other organizing traumatic dynamics, *betrayal* and *stigmatization*, also operate for boys in terms of seeking out partners to "divert themselves" of their self-image by humiliating and initiating others, perversely treating the others as "things" as they had been. This becomes instituted as part of the cycle, and there are ample models in societal views of the appropriateness of women and children as victims.

Finkelhor (1984) described the pre-conditions for abusive behaviour, including traumatic conditioning factors that account for a sexual-interest arousal to a child; factors that "release" or trigger such responses in the young person or adult (e.g. drugs, alcohol); factors that bring the potential abusers and child together and which fail to protect; and factors in the child that make him or her vulnerable.

The victim response to sexual abuse

The victim response to sexual abuse emerges from the immediate post-traumatic effects, and from longer-term traumagenic responses given the length of time that children are often abused over. The responses of boys have been described above.

Girls adopt a more internalizing mode as a result of their sexualization and powerlessness. They feel that the abuse must be their fault, reinforced by the adults' justifications that children like "sexual" attention. Girls develop highly negative self attributes which they struggle to deal with by self-mutilation, anorectic patterns, clinging to their abuser—even "falling in love" or finding unsuitable partners or adopting promiscuous roles, which then justifies the abuser—or develop "multiple-personalities" with false selves to gain some degree of control. Lorraine, described in chapter four, is an example of this.

Louise was 14 years old, the daughter of two pre-lingually deaf parents, who revealed the long-standing abuse by her father when he started to initiate anal abuse. She then spoke to her teacher in school. The father accepted responsibility for the abuse but was convinced that the sexual activities were 50:50—as much desired by Louise as by himself. He had convinced himself that her lack of response—the passive-victim response—signalled consent. She was in fact abstracting, and removing herself from the experience in a self-induced hypnotic state.

She was asked about her traumatic responses, flash-backs.

Therapist: Do you have any pictures in your mind—when you are falling asleep, or when you see your dad?

Louise: Well I am a girl who likes to dream up fantasy, sort of believe in it, and I'm falling asleep I have a picture of a monster killing a girl.

Therapist: Doing sexual things like dad?

Louise: Yes, that's right.

Therapist: With your father's face?

Louise: You've got it exactly.

It is important to note that I was using my knowledge of flash-backs, of re-enactment processes, to name them. An active "assumptive" naming-and-bringing-forth approach is essential to confront and help traumatized individuals know they are not alone. The most difficult aspect of traumatic-sexualization effects to "bring forth" is the sexual responses in the child. A sexual reaction frequently makes the child feel that she initiated the traumatizing action and the other must have known she would respond. It is a great relief when this can be broached in a girl's therapeutic group. They can then realize that they are physiologically sexually responsive beings and that the abuser's actions and their responses are not on the same level.

A further aspect of *sexualization* and *powerlessness* amongst girls is the process elaborating and recreating an abusive context. Lorraine (chapter four) described the way she could semi-hypnotize herself, stare into space, and elaborate abusive actions by a wide variety of people in her life. She felt that in another part of her mind she knew this was not true, but at the time she felt confused about what was real or not. It is not surprising such young woman are labelled hysterical, psychiatric, borderline, and so forth. They create different selves to cope—e.g. strong selves, scatty selves, selves with various names—to develop a variety of ways of being in control.

Louise decided that she was going to be a lorry driver when she left school—her father's job. She had adopted a forceful, quite masculine style of dress; she had decided she was not going to have boy friends. She wanted absolutely nothing to do with her father and was not interested in therapy. She had clearly adopted a highly independent mode, which in some ways maintained the parental role she had in the family as the hearing first-born of two deaf parents. She was literally their link with the world and had been forced into a premature adult role, including an expectation that she would be her father's partner.

The complexity of the traumatization response has been recently revealed with the association now shown between the anorectic response and abuse. Post-traumatic responses can affect eating in a variety of ways, e.g. through association with oral abuse. The need to adopt less-invasive techniques in the treatment of anorexia is now clear, e.g. being aware that family meals can maintain an abusive pattern when parents are asked to feed their resistant daughters. There is a need to carry out individual investigations in such conditions to exclude hidden abusive behaviour.

The process of traumatization and its effects

Figure 5 demonstrates the overall process. Traumatic stress appears as a first-level response, and traumagenic dynamics effects as a second-level response. Both of these impact on developmental and interactional processes. Responses are defined as internalizing or externalizing to reflect female- and male-mode responses. The notion of "mode" is introduced to indicate that girls or boys may follow gender-biased "socially constructed" pathways. Attachments, attributional set, identification, rôle, and behavioural responses are then described in broadly internalizing or externalizing forms. The system is seen as containing a feed-back loop, since the responses to original traumatic and stressful events in turn evoke—and involve the individual in—events that may further traumatize and maintain the system.

Sexual abuse and interlocking roles

There is considerable controversy about the "interlocking" roles in sexual abuse. Men may justify their abusive actions by blaming their partners' "failures" for their sexually abusive orientations. Do they "find" vulnerable partners, or are they "sought" by partners who have themselves been abused? Is there a complementary fit of perpetrator and victim? Alternatively do men with abusive orientations choose vulnerable partners or single mothers with children of particular ages and organize their partners' and children's victim roles?

Our own recently completed research (Monck et al., 1991) revealed that a considerable proportion (43%) of the mothers of children who were abused had themselves been abused; also 20% or 30% of those men who abused subsequently admitted to abuse in childhood. Both the abusers and the mothers had very mixed care in childhood, and many men and women had few good memories of their childhood. Over a third of the mothers could not bring themselves to believe that their children had been abused by their partner, and they supported the parent who denied responsibility. Indeed, only about 9% of the abusers properly took responsibility for their abuse.

The reasons such parents came together—who influenced whom and in what way—were very varied indeed. There were examples

FIGURE 5. *The process of traumatization*

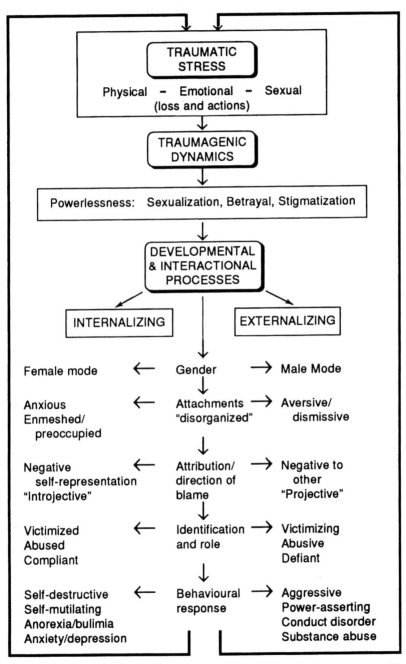

of couples who had long-standing complementary roles, others where current situations brought forward an abusive orientation that may well have been latent in the man due to early emotional, physical, or sexual abuse. There were also situations where a man with a long-standing abusive orientation had targeted and groomed a particular child or children, and found a vulnerable family.

Recent research has compared family-interaction patterns in families where sexual abuse had occurred with non-abusive families (Madonna, Scoyk, & Jones, 1990). The research indicated a rigidity of beliefs in abusive families, a failure to allow children to have an individual voice; rather, they were expected to comply with family norms. Parents were emotionally unavailable for children, adults were more focused on themselves than on their children, and there was a general instability and poor family and marital functioning.

Whatever the specific patterns, there is no doubt about the vulnerability of the mothers of children who became abused or of the traumatic experiences in the childhood of men who abuse.

Traumatic effects on children are related not only to how extensively they have been abused, e.g. abuse with penetration, but also whether they were believed, supported, and warmly nurtured by their caring parent. Older girls were *less* likely to be believed, and are more likely to be rejected and blamed. Such responses deepen traumatic effects already caused by being directly abused, creating yet more vulnerable young people and, in turn, parents.

Figure 6 describes common systemic patterns associated with sexual abuse. The communication arrows bending back on themselves indicate that communications signalling distress or anger, which should modify the actions of the other, are re-labelled as the child deserving abusive action and rejection.

THE TRAUMA-ORGANIZED SYSTEM OF VIOLENCE BETWEEN PARTNERS—WIFE BATTERING

To be a battered wife is defined as one who receives deliberate, severe, and repeated injury from her husband, involving punching with a closed fist and more severe forms of violence.

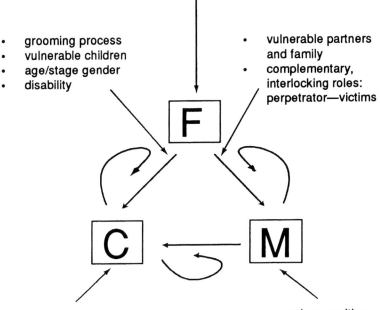

FIGURE 6. *Attributions of physical sexual abuse*
(C = child; F = father; M = mother)

Blaming mode/silencing strategies:
—abusive actions justified by blaming partners
and children's behaviour
—partners and children organized into victim role

- grooming process
- vulnerable children
- age/stage gender
- disability

- vulnerable partners
  and family
- complementary,
  interlocking roles:
  perpetrator—victims

F

C ⇄ M

- traumatic responses
  re-labelled as deserving
  abusive action
- self-blame/re-enactment
  of victimization
- silencing
- guilt

- powerless position
- perceptions
  organized to reject
  child, and blame
  self
- re-enactment of
  victim roles

Rape in partnerships can occur (see Carmel, in chapter four) and is either one aspect of a violent response or a result of perverse sexual orientation.

Gender issues
and the trauma-organized systems of battering

Goldner et al. (1990) have recently described their attempt to make sense of the processes involved in violence between men and women. They felt that the development of gender differences represented a key. They pointed out that gender perceptions and development of self-perceptions occur at the same developmental phase. They felt that the primary identity of the child is co-created from a series of conflict-layered internal self-representations for boys and girls.

We have already seen the way that "gender self-representations" and responses to the traumatic experiences of sexual abuse can result in differential abusive responses in boys and girls. Through such abusive enactments, boys "divest" themselves of traumatic responses and hand them on. Girls take a more passive identification, see themselves as responsible, punish themselves, and take on victim roles.

Goldner and her colleagues point out that boys are familiar with the process of constructing themselves from a negative—what they are not, not being the mother, not being the victim—and taking on the exact opposite role. For boys and men, the threat is being reminded of powerlessness, a powerlessness that is also associated with the maternal bond. Women are seen as reminders of what had to be given up; a child reminds them of their vulnerability and victimization. Violence and abuse is then used as an illusory way of gaining control and autonomy and reversing powerlessness.

Ali was the partner of Carmel, the abused woman described in chapter four. He talked about himself as the spoilt, indulged golden boy of his family; he described his parents and sisters dancing to his every need. He even talked about himself as a "millionaire in training". His marriage to a compliant partner bored him; he was excited by Carmel, whom he saw as a lively, independent, worldly woman, more of a match for the man who has to *be* everything, *have* everything. In reality his "omnipotence" is created by the *other's* perception of him rather than his own sense of reality. I have already described Carmel's compliance, and her attempt and training to fit into the other's need, sharing with his wife, adopting his name, and changing her children's name to his.

She was fitting, in an extreme form, into the girl's role as described by Goldner, seeing herself as part of the mother's psychological space—to become empathic, to become the power behind the throne, the object of desire, subject as object, self through the regard of the other. Her abuse by her brother and contempt by her mother locked her into this role, which she re-enacted with other partners and with Ali.

So how does violence arise in this context where it appears that each partner fulfils the other's needs, and struggles to give everything, be everything? Ali complained that he "tried to please" both his wife and Carmel, by working all hours to keep both partners and his two sons which each of the women bore him at the same time. He exhausted himself; surely, he felt, he *must* be everything to them, giving everything, being everything, everything they could need or desire.

Although Carmel could live with a partial illusion of the golden reality he painted for her, the reality of her position, her loneliness, broke through and she attempted to expand her life by renewing old links with another partner. This shattered the illusion for Ali. Awareness of her actions clearly evoked his sense of insecurity. Seeing Carmel acting independently broke through to the insecurity behind the illusion of the golden boy who was either everything or nothing. Echoes are evoked of the woman/mother who had to be given up, despite appearing to think of him as everything. He used violence as the illusory, or permitted, way in social patriarchal contexts to gain personal power and autonomy. He was absolutely *certain* that she had abandoned him and was starting another affair. This justified his grievance to himself, aroused a "right" to be indignant, humiliate her, beat her, bind her, gag her, and abuse her sexually. Inhibitions were unnecessary, care was redundant.

Her response was to feel he was justified, but that he had no right to be "the executioner". The scene is set for reconciliation, redemption, for Carmel to rescue him from his abject guilt and from the police action which threatened. She had already withdrawn actions against him previously, and the scene was set for a cycle of forgiveness, a honeymoon, and later renewed violence when the balance was pushed out of kilter once more.

There are, of course, many other factors entering into the couple's violence from their personal histories and context. However, the strength of the tie between the two, the magic of their sense of redemption, as Goldner described, is all pervasive and is the secret that binds, despite pain, as each re-enacts a powerful interlocking story and maintains it.

CHAPTER SIX

Trauma-organized systems: breaking the denial process by externalizing

TRAUMA-ORGANIZED SYSTEMS AND INTERNALIZING CONVERSATIONS

The essence of trauma-organized systems is that they are focused on *action*, not *talking* or *thinking*. Victimizing activities are justified by construing some action or aspect of the victim as causal and justifying abusive action, whether physical, sexual, or emotional. The impulses to hit, to be sexual, or to criticize are felt to be overwhelming, out of the victimizer's control, "stronger" than him or her, described as a reflex response, with no time for thought.

Attributing the cause to the victim—as justifying punishment, sexual action, hurt—then justifies the loss of control and disinhibition of violent action. This scenario, of course, becomes a repetitive one and shapes the attitudes and responses of victimizer and victim, and builds into what White, linked to Brunner's views on action and meaning, described as a "dominant story" (White, 1989) and we described as *common* and *intersubjective meanings* (Kinston & Bentovim, 1980). White describes this dominant story as emerging

51

from "internalizing conversations", which victimizer and victim alike develop to make some sense of earlier and current experiences. Similarly, individuals in the context who might take a protective role develop their own "story" influenced by their own experience and by the victimizer or victim.

The victimizer blots out and deletes his actions as forcefully as the traumatized individuals and avoids thinking, talking, or being reminded of his or her abuse as if the reality of action is negated. This is essential to avoid guilt and a sense of responsibility, and an alternative story is developed, e.g. never to abuse again, or even think that it did not happen. Yet the context that arouses the abusive action remains; the urge may be felt as addictive, arousing a sense of helplessness. Punishment may be expected, yet arousal and action recurs; relief follows briefly, which maintains the abusive impulse. If discovered the abuser reconstructs his own reality to feel a victim of society, a victim of his uncontrolled impulses, a victim of the child who describes his abusive action, a victim of the professional who gets the child to speak. He rapidly engages others in his construction—and there are many in the extended family or in the media who are willing to be recruited to believe his word against the weak word of women and children, who are seen as "incapable of truth".

The ability of such beliefs to organize the very thinking processes of the individual who has been abused can be very powerful. Victims come to doubt their own experiences, begin to wonder if their abuse was reality or fantasy. The danger of re-victimization by the family and societal agencies is very powerful as a dominant story that negates the victim's sense of reality. The victim develops his or her own dominant story to account for the abuse, feels responsible for the victimizer, and constructs a story with a sense of poor self-worth, deserving of abuse and punishment, or else a sense of outrage and wish to retaliate.

EXTERNALIZING CONVERSATIONS

To counter these organizing stories it is necessary to engage in *externalizing conversations* between the therapist and the individual or family. This generates what Michael White and David Epston (1989) have described as counter- or anti-language. Problems are objectified, put outside the self through hypothetical questions, future questions, circular questions, the use of "dolls" of the self rather than the self, the objectification of the abusive or victim self.

There is then the possibility of developing an alternative and preferred knowledge separate from the "dominant" stories that constitute their lives and are constructed from traumatizing and traumatic responses. Alternative stories have to be constructed which separate the individual from the activities in which he or she has been enmeshed. This is illustrated in the following examples.

A serious abuser: Mr A

Mr A had abused his two stepchildren, for which he had served a lengthy prison sentence. Throughout he had attempted to get a re-trial as his dominant story was that he was convinced that there had been a miscarriage of justice—although his barrister advised him against this re-trial as he felt the result might be a lengthier prison sentence. After his period in prison he wanted to return to live with his partner and the children he had abused and his own younger children he had not abused. He was aware that Social Services, exercising their protective role, would oppose this on the proper grounds that a man who had abused children, who was not taking responsibility, could not be "in control" of his impulse and could give no assurance of future protection of children in his care.

We saw the family prior to the court case to test these issues. The children on separate interviews had no difficulty convincing us of the abuse through the detailed account they gave. The mother believed the children but wanted to believe her partner.

Mr A was aware of the issues and begged us to hypnotize him so that he could prove he had not abused the children. We asked him what his response would be if he discovered that he "had" in fact abused them—he hotly denied the possibility. We pressed with hypothetical questions. Such questions "externalize" the issues by asking such questions as, "*If* you remembered, *if* you thought that you might have, *if* you knew you had, *if* your wife knew, *if* the court knew, *if* you woke up one morning suddenly 'knowing' that you had abused, how would you respond?" His immediate response, in common with so many men, was "I would top myself—commit suicide". He could not tolerate the self-loathing and hatred of the action which at one moment was denied, yet earlier whilst in progress must have been "constructed" as reasonable and appropriate, and then "deconstructed" as never having happened. If he acknowledged his actions, he feared exclusion, abandonment, and self-hatred. Life would not be worth living.

We did hypnotize him, and as we regressed him towards the time he was living with the family he became profoundly depressed, so we stopped the process. Such a procedure supported the chain of questioning which ended in the "I would top myself" response. The following creates an "alternative" story to justify the deletion:

"Would it be better not to know, because if the court believed your daughter, could a man who did not know he had abused a child ever be trusted?"

"Do you feel a man who abused children *could* ever be trusted?"

"If there is a grain of truth, could you as a man undertake a mission to develop a more caring, respectful view of children, or would it be impossible to live with yourself?"

These questions help test whether the individual has the strength to face the reality of his actions and construct the stark truth of his actions and their origin. As another approach, an alternative story may be mobilized to spare the child from having to subscribe to a story of blame and poor self-regard.

The following case illustrates the trauma-organized family belief system and attempts to externalize the situation.

A sexually abused stepdaughter: Tracy

Tracy, a 14-year-old, had been seriously abused sexually by her stepfather. A criminal court had allowed Tracy's stepfather to spend evenings at his own home provided that he slept at his mother's home. Social Services had attempted to explore how Tracy felt, but the girl said she was happy for him to be there; her mother indicated the need for his support with younger children, and her forgiveness of her husband's actions.

On individual interview we asked Tracy how she managed to live with him when there must be flash-backs and memories of his abusive rape of her. The abuse had been violent, and she had raced bleeding to a neighbour. She told us she had constructed a very different story and developed an "internal conversation", that the rape had not been committed by her stepfather but by a stranger who had broken into her home. So she did not connect the abuse with her stepfather. Such "conversations" are similar to those that arise and trigger the deletion and dissociation responses seen after serious trauma. They have some similarities to a self-induced hypnotic status, and they may also induce the multiple disconnected conversations of the "multiple personality".

Using a "future" orientated question to externalize the issue, we asked what might happen one day if she dropped this construction, how she would feel about her stepfather. She could not answer this. We wondered whether she might feel angry, murderous towards him, or whether she would have to avoid such a feeling forever, "sacrifice herself" because of her mother's need for her father. We tried to find out what might help develop a conversation nearer reality, as we were concerned about how her current "story" might affect future relationships.

The stepfather had developed an agoraphobic state and could not be seen by ourselves or other therapeutic agencies. He had developed a lived-out dominant "story" for himself which deprived him both of his liberty and of having to think about his options. The suspended sentence he received gave no mandate for treatment, and he was at home to such an extent that there was no motivation for a treatment process that would have meant facing actions, thinking, talking, and acknowledgement—a different sort of alternative story construction. The family had "achieved" almost everything, apart from him sleeping at home. The girl and her mother refused to attend for treatment on a voluntary basis—we and Social Services felt powerless, despite our concerns for the girl's future. The mother was organized by the father's minimization of the abuse and the girl's apparent "neutral" response to her stepfather.

Our view is that the only way to undo the system organized by traumatic events is to "deconstruct" the "organized" traumatic system, and resulting dominant story, by attending groups and doing therapeutic work, and by holding conversations that talk about actions, experiences, feelings rather than delete them, and establish an alternative story that reflects reality in thought. To help family members face the process, the return of a child, of a parent, or of a partner may need to be conditional on successfully working at such problems.

The following case is an example of a "family" process organizing the response to a traumatic event.

A trauma-organized system: the T family

Observing family processes can demonstrate the way traumatic actions are processed and result in characteristic family conversations. Initially there was a first meeting when Mr. T, the father, met the three children he had abused, girls of 13, 15, and 17 years of age; a daughter of 19 and a son of 11 he had not abused. He came from prison for the day, and I wanted him to acknowledge that although it was painful to be in prison his children should not feel guilty for having spoken. They had constructed a story in which they were the guilty party, not he. I said that some men felt on reflection that prison, whilst a punishment, was helpful as it gave them time to think and, by implication, to face the true story of their actions.

He said his children should not feel guilty; he was at fault, not them—they had never done anything to encourage his sexual interest in them. But prison was the wrong place for a man like him (whatever that meant). He supported them yet disqualified them at the same time.

The 13-year-old daughter began sobbing; the mother, who was gazing into her husband's eyes, stopped her husband's comforting gesture and said it was alright to cry, she was only young. Her sisters tried to comfort her but again the mother stopped them, more harshly this time: "Let her cry, she's only young." The family lapsed into silence, the younger child sobbing without being comforted. My attempt to "externalize" conversations and co-create a different reality and story—which included the need to acknowledge guilt, pain, and responsibility—had been blocked. The mother had been abused extensively—she blamed herself for not meeting her husband's sexual needs. The dominating story, which included her responsibility and by implication the children's, was reinforced. She could not protect her daughter or acknowledge her distress, and there was silence where there should have been sharing and support.

Later the family did a family task interview to explore the way they interacted without a therapist present. They were asked to discuss what family members were like. An idealistic picture emerged as the mother held onto her husband's hand, orchestrating the response of family members. A story emerged of a successful family: how well they were doing at school, in social relationships, in work. They were clearly addressing the camera, to convince the unseen audience of their closeness, their trustworthiness, how little this man's extensive abuse had affected them. They needed him, or at least the mother needed him; he needed the mother and the children to need him. This organized and constructed a family picture of good relatedness, centred on the mother orchestrating the responses in their family task.

Such patterns have now persuaded us that individual work with family members, preferably in peer groups, are essential if such a process is to be confronted and individuals helped to be able to construct a different reality and a different story within the family. The model of group work, with family work interspersed to test and give opportunities for trying a different mode of relating and co-constructing a different story developed from each peer group, seems to be a useful approach. The therapists need to be active to help family members use their resources to create new external conversations and a new reality in their families rather than confirm the old.

CONFRONTING TRAUMA-ORGANIZED SYSTEMS

I have already indicated how hypothetical questions name and externalize the traumatic processes. This helps confront avoidance and deletion; abusive acts can be thought about and re-enacted in a safe context, so that the original event can be named and the process of therapeutic work initiated.

For sexually and physically abused children, the use of anatomic dolls has been invaluable. Abused children play spontaneously and can *"externalize"* their experience by playing out with dolls that trigger reminders.

Katie was a 4½-year-old who was placed in foster care when her drug-abusing mother left her alone in a flat with her younger siblings. Within the foster family she began to behave in a highly sexualized way in her play with other children, and with the foster parents. When seen for an assessment interview she was left with the undressed anatomic dolls

A typical pattern of behaviour with the dolls was observed. She initially showed an aversion to the dolls and said she wanted to put their clothes on, but she was encouraged to play with them, and it was noted that there was a response like a flash-back of action. She handled the male doll's penis, pulled it, and then picked up the doll and said forcefully, "There's a winkie coming". She thrust the doll on top of the child doll, squashed their genitals together, picked them up, and then made some obviously orgiastic-sounding noises as she rubbed them violently together. Then suddenly the episode seemed terminated. She put the dolls down, turned away, and went to another part of the room.

This episode is very similar to a flash-back of memory, but in this child it became a flash of action. Given a context that reminded her of the original traumatic experience, she may have had a flash-back or reminder which organized her to cross a boundary of resistance to enactment.

THE USE OF DOLLS IN INTERVIEWING TO "EXTERNALIZE" TRAUMATIC ACTIVITIES

Fiona, aged 9 years, was not living with her parents when we saw her. We asked her why this was the case, and she said it was because of the things that her father had done. She welcomed using the anatomical dolls to show us what had happened. She laid the father doll without trousers on top of the little girl doll, representing herself. But she seized up, became frozen, and seemed unable to continue. Getting close to the actual memory of the experience that triggered intense feelings produced a paralysed deletion response.

We asked whether she could show what had happened by describing the action using the dolls; she still remained frozen. It is necessary to construct a dialogue and develop the story of actions with her and co-create a reality that had been deleted. To achieve this, the therapist then took the father doll away, pointed to the little girl doll, and asked her where was she hurt. Fiona could point to the vaginal area. She was asked what hurt her, and she felt empowered to point to the penis of the father doll. Did she like it? "No it was horrible."

These were the first words to fill the hole in her mind, the beginning of a language of words to describe her overwhelming affects which led to the dissociation. With encouragement, using the dolls to speak, she could enact the experience, describe the erection, the movement, the place where she was hurt, the memories that broke through when she was trying to sleep. A conversation is started and, through describing detailed feelings, the actions themselves could be stated and her story put into words. Her knowledge was unique and could not be "imagined" without experience. In a context where there was active listening, the development of conversation without silencing threats could occur. It was possible to initiate the emotional processing of experiences, to co-construct a safer world where thoughts without action could be shared and anxious responses dispersed. An alternative story could be constructed.

EXTERNALIZING ABUSIVE ACTIVITIES

Naming abusive actions to "externalize" and confront realities is an important process, e.g. the notion of the "germ of truth" introduced by Alan Jenkins (Jenkins, 1990). Abusive individuals are frequently only ever able to admit to a small proportion of the reality of their abusive activities as so many of them are deleted, to avoid guilt, fear of retaliation, and punishment. In working with young offenders or adult offenders, sheets of paper can be used for the whole group to delineate the steps towards abusive actions. The contribution of a small step from each can co-create a consensus reality of what occurred. Each individual can see the cycle written up, and be asked how much of this applies to them. A questionnaire can be constructed which incorporates the whole system; written down, the information may be easier to confront and easier for the individual to accept ownership. An external alternative story can be written which faces the truth for each, and helps create "safe" knowledge rather than dangerous ignorance.

Talking about the "force", the "other me", the nasty one who takes over, "make suggestions about what to do, where to go, who to choose, what to do", are all helpful ways of co-constructing external conversation. Michael White's notions of "externalizing" the temper that influences the child, and causes the whole family to be angry and punitive, can be used with great effect in helping abusers think about the violent, inconsiderate, uncaring individual who takes them over and who needs controlling. Once this "external" story is accepted. the individual can take the step of creating a story that includes the origins of these actions, not excludes them.

The victim can be helped to think of abuse as something being put into them, taking them over, making them remember, think, or try to run away from situations where it may be met again. This also help victims and perpetrators to take control and actualize and develop their caring or competent self to develop an alternative story of control. They may need to discover the "unique outcomes" that represent the times they responded differently, developed a different conversation, learnt to acknowledge, value, and develop their resources, not denigrate and feel powerless to resist endless repetition.

EXTERNALIZING PROCESSES IN PHYSICAL ABUSE

Previously we accepted that one may be able to work therapeutically without knowing exactly who perpetrated a particular physically abusive episode, such as which parent actually hit the child. This is not an acceptable view currently. One mother, a nurse, created a story that if her husband knew she had hit their child, she would be left and abandoned by him. Therefore she had to deny all knowledge of how her son was hurt.

It would have been possible to have worked with her, "collude" with her denial, and support the obvious competent care she demonstrated. But without defining the abusive process, it would be impossible to ensure the safety of the child at a point of future stress.

Using an approach which "assumed" her responsibility, she revealed that she had felt abandoned herself, as her parents had died at about the time of her own child's birth. They had made a suicide pact in the face of one of them having a fatal illness. Feeling an "abandoned" child herself, she could not bear the demands for care in the crying of her own child—which reminded her of her own abandoned-self story. She had to silence the crying and her action was to shake the baby, which caused a sub-dural effusion and brain swelling. She had to "co-create" and externalize her story with her therapist, and then with her husband, before it was safe to return the child to her care.

The process of exploring parents' feelings that *they* are the abused child when they are dealing with their distressed children or partners is an important route to externalizing the "victimizing" process.

Another man said that if he acknowledged that he might have shaken his baby, who had subsequently died, he could never trust himself with another child. Yet if he did not confront his actions, how could anybody trust him? This is a dilemma that has to be grasped and may result in a connotation that to deny may be a way of ensuring the safety of a future child, since a court could not trust the child with that parent. How could someone who did not know about his or her anger ever know what might provoke it in the future, and therefore how could he or she ever be trusted?

We recently saw a couple, now in their 30s, whose first child had died as a result of a shake injury when they were much younger, she 17 and he 16. Subsequently, a further child suffered a leg fracture; also, two children were removed at birth. They then did some work on their problems as a couple, hoping to keep their current child. They were seen late in the pregnancy.

This quite mature couple had now dealt with a number of issues between themselves, including marital violence. But they could not bring themselves to believe that they had caused the injuries. They blamed the nursery, the hospital, to try to develop a story that could encompass their actions. Using an externalizing mode, we asked if they could put themselves back into the frame of being 16 or 17 years old and remember how they would have felt when their baby cried, struggled during changing, fussing—not now in their 30s— but then, as teenagers. Could they imagine seizing a kicking leg and pulling it on the changing mat, being furious at having their sleep disturbed, shaking the baby to stop the crying which felt like an accusation, and even getting momentary satisfaction?

Using our knowledge to reconstruct a likely scenario and putting this couple back in touch with experiences that were "de-constructed" helped them to separate their "caring responsible selves" from the impulsive teenagers they had been, and begin to face their responsibilities.

USE OF STORY STEMS

A similar technique which brings forth the meaning from experiences of young children between the ages of 3 and 7 years is the use of a "story stem". Using miniature dolls or animals, a variety of stories are started which the child then completes (Main, 1991; Hodges, 1991). Story stems were introduced as a way for children to use various stories as narratives to develop their own story, reflecting their own way of processing their experiences and particularly their attachments. An example would be a family of animals, e.g. pigs. The little pig gets lost—what would happen, would the mother or father find her or would she be lost for ever, or would another animal find her? The narratives that children develop reflect accurately their attachment patterns.

Katherine, a 5-year-old, living with her mother and stepfather, a possible abuser, presented with what sounded like a story constructed by her mother, that her father, who saw her at weekends, was the one who had been abusing her. Initially she created a spontaneous story about her daddy, Stan, who was bad because he touched her; she had a secret place where she could hide when her father climbed into the room. Then her mummy and (step) daddy, Harry, fought him and he went away. This was a story rattled off with little affect. She added that mummy had told her that daddy Stan hurt her, and that daddy Harry had done nothing wrong.

There were few protective parental figures: in her responses to the story stems the little girl in the stories was rescued by magic—animals were able to fly, parents were uninvolved or absent.

She then developed a story out of a stem that involved being taken to hospital. She played with intense concentration and seriousness. She needed a hiding place as mummy and daddy Harry were "going to get her" to sell her. She built a strong barrier around the doll representing herself, to hide from her parents. At the point when the Harry doll was to find her the game disintegrated and she had to go to the toilet. She thus presented a picture of insecure attachments, not being able to turn to the maternal figure.

These are forms of conversations and examination of stories appropriate to the age of the child and her stage of development. Spontaneous play has always been seen as a way of "conversing" for younger children; structured approaches to interviewing

(Vizard & Tranter, 1988) or the use of story stems gives some structure to exploring experiences and current stories by triggering memories. The development of alternative stories will be seen to be the key to the successful processing of abusive experiences (see chapter eight).

CHAPTER SEVEN

A focal model
to encompass the descriptions of
the trauma-determined family system

Although family issues have been brought into the case examples given previously, it is important to be able to develop an approach that will enable the therapist to develop a systematic way of describing families and planning therapeutic work. Families construct a multitude of stories and meanings from the individual and shared experiences that make up family life.

In families where violence is occurring we are interested to explore the current victimizer and victim stories, and to examine the potential for developing alternative stories and realities that will reverse current and future abusive potential. Hopefully this will assist individuals to emerge from their families with a potential for healthy relating rather than living out a traumatic reality that remains a live story instead of becoming a past story.

The "focal approach" (Bentovim & Kinston, 1991) is one that fits this need; in this approach, traumatic events are considered to be the prime initiator of disturbances, associated with intense anxiety and helplessness.

The family, viewed as a human system, is embedded in a social context; culture is a critical constraint; and purposes, feelings, and meanings—stories—are critical factors. The approach is developmentally orientated and considers the health of the family in the context of its life cycle within and across generations. Therapeutic work has to change the patterns of action involved in abusive activities, as well as meanings and stories relating to them. In other words, family members need to change their way of being, and to gain an understanding of how the dysfunction arose that created a meaningful story for victim and victimizer and protective parent alike.

An essential component of working with families, and developing a meaningful systemic approach to violence within the family, is to develop a satisfactory way of describing and assessing families. Although some family therapists have argued that description is the antithesis of treatment, it is our opinion that inquiry and understanding is the necessary prerequisite to deliberate action. Therefore a detailed inquiry about the family is the essential base for meaningful therapeutic work.

It is generally accepted that systemic epistemology, and systems description, is the essential basis for family therapy. In our view it is essential to provide a framework for family description which is meaningful for both therapists and researchers (Kinston & Bentovim, 1990).

The family description format and framework, which we developed, grew out of practice. Generally speaking, family therapists make three types or tiers of description, each of which subsumes the former. The *first tier* focuses on *aspects of family interaction* and was never called systemic. The *second tier* focused on *patterns* or *sequences* or *conversation* and *actions* involving the whole family and was usually held to be *systemic*. The *third tier* placed whatever was seen in a broader or *narrower context*, to guide therapy, and was also referred to as systemic.

When we examined and analysed these tiers we saw that each contained two levels, and we also realized that we had to attempt to describe how a family might be in the future. Figure 6 shows the resulting family descriptive framework that we (Kinston & Bentovim, 1990) have produced and also the nature of the inquiring system implied by the particular level.

FIGURE 6.   *Framework for family description*

Level	Family Description	Inquiring system
L1	Concepts of Interaction (self-evident, enduring) = ideas about family Interaction and life Needed to organize observations	Formal-analytic (resolution into simple elements)
L2	Items of Interaction Actual concrete items of Interactions. Simplest account of things which are clinically recognizable	Empirical (acting on observation)
L3	Episodes of Interaction First contextual organization of L1 and L2 into episodes which involve whole family.	Synthetic (putting parts together to make a whole)
L4	Patterns of Meaning This description places family episodes in context using past family history, etc., to enable an increased understanding	Dialectical (meaning of any reality is to be found in the opposites which constitute it)
L5	Holistic Formulation Provides a single complete account of how the family is now	Systemic (conducted according to complex whole)
L6	Type Formulation A type of family to which the actual family more or less conforms based on one or more features which are held to be characteristic	Dialogic (talking)
L7	Requisition Formulation Idealistic. A conception of the family as it might be if therapy is successful.	Contemplative (thinking)

Our proposed framework for description consists of a system of seven hierarchical levels. Although one has to present them progressively from Level 1 to Level 7, each contains and implies the other. All levels are implicit, and a description at any one level confirms the other; no level is intrinsically more important than any other, although levels do appear to reflect a progressively integrated comprehensiveness to description, and there is a progressive increase in contextualisation.

The lower five levels are descriptions of the actual family being observed or emerging from his conversation with them, whereas the upper two levels are descriptions of the potential—the way the family could be categorized, or could become with therapeutic work.

Level 1—Concepts of interaction

Level 1 descriptions are the concepts or ideas about family interaction and family life without which even the simplest objective description—let alone the necessary complex account required for therapy—is absolutely impossible. Without concepts to organize observations, a family interview is a complex jumble of phenomena; the observer feels lost and unable to know how and where to direct his or her attention.

Concepts are part of the experts' specialized language and are important for comparison of families and to describe the family being encountered. When we are considering the issue of family violence, concepts also need to encompass not only the family we are concerned with, but also the fact that the family has often become embedded and caught up within the social and professional context, including the family therapist if brought in to assess or treat.

One could argue that there is no such thing as a violent family, only the family as defined by the professional who has recognized it. Concepts are therefore an imposition on reality, not inherent or to be taken for granted. The aim of conceptualizing is to reduce confusion and permit communication. Therefore, the associated inquiring system is the *formal-analytic*, or *rationalistic-deductive*. Inquiring depends on the logical development and analysis of concepts, to be judged by criteria of coherence and consistency.

Concepts applicable to the description of families may be either elemental or global. An elemental concept might be "interruption", "laughter", and "direct disagreement". Examples of global concepts are "boundaries" and "parenting". Both forms are taken to be self-evident and are assumed to be enduring features of families.

A number of domains in the family therapy field have been identified and analysed. Loader et al. (1981) and Kinston, Loader, and Miller (1987) have described the main domains as: the *affective life* of the family; *communication, boundaries, alliances, adaptability,* and *stability* of family organization; and *competence* for family tasks and relationships with the environment. These can be subdivided into sub-domains and can be the basis of ways of deriving a consensus about the degree of concern there should be about the family. Figure 7 (after Kinston et al., 1987) gives an idea of the way one area can be conceptualized in the form of a scale. The alliance area is a key to help make sense of families where violence occurs. The family is conceptualized as being at *breakdown point, dysfunctional, adequate,* or *optimal.* Once the clinician has his set of concepts and how they are defined, it then becomes necessary to focus on actual events in detail. This takes us to a second level.

Level 2—Items of interaction

These are the actual concrete items of interaction and are the simplest account of things or events that are clinically recognizable in a particular case. The event may be either verbal or non-verbal: for example, an actual interruption, a particular hostile gesture, an identifiable agreement or disagreement, a given promise. Inevitably such items are not at all simple; they may be evaluated, but no item on its own can be construed as the family being functional or dysfunctional in the total family context. Indeed, when stripped of context such items make little sense. Items, however, are simple, relatively unambiguous, apparently objective, and suited to obtaining reliability; they often serve as an ideal base for empirical inquiry.

But the meaning content of items is low, and it is difficult to interpret accumulated data. To illustrate this, two cases will be described where a number of "items" occurred.

The first is an example of a physically abused, neglected child who had a period of failure to thrive. A baby girl of 10 months, Hava had been physically abused, including skull fracture, but the very young parents denied knowledge of how this could have occurred. When seen she was being cared for by the maternal grandmother and grandfather who had put themselves forward as alternative carers. We were asked to assess the child's future needs, and the following items were noted:

Therapist: Why were you put in prison?

FIGURE 7.   Family health—alliances—considering

	Breakdown	Dysfunctional
PATTERN OF RELATIONSHIPS	Serious deficiencies; marked splits, scapegoating, severe triangulation, or isolation of all family members.	Serious discord or distance between members, or shifting or exclusive alignments. Children repeatedly detour parental tension or conflicts.
MARITAL RELATIONSHIP	Destructive relationship, eg. couple fused, at war, or isolated from one another.	Overt marital difficulties; or both partners dissatisfied.
PARENTAL RELATIONSHIP	Parents not working together at all, or extremely weak, divisive, or conflicted relationship.	Parents repeatedly disagree, act without reference to one another, or one parent repeatedly takes over or opts out.
PARENT–CHILD RELATIONSHIP	Both parents reject, ignore, exploit, continuously attack, or disqualify a child.	Parental attitudes and behaviours are clearly unsupportive or harmful; poor understanding of the children.
CHILD–PARENT RELATIONSHIP	Children avoid, reject, continually oppose, or cling to parent(s); or show marked differentiation in their attitudes to each parent.	One or more children show oppositional, withdrawn, over-dependent, or domineering behaviour towards (parent(s).
SIBLING RELATIONSHIPS	Siblings fight continuously or ignore each other; extreme rivalry and competition for the parents' attention	Obvious discord or distance between the siblings.

70

relationships and coalitions among family members

Adequate	Optimal
Satisfactory relationships but with greater closeness or distance between some family members than others.	The nature and strength of relationships between family members is constructive and appropriate to their respective ages and roles.
Basically satisfactory with some areas of discontent.	Mature relationship; warm, supportive, affectionate, empathic, compatible; couple work together well.
Basic agreement on child-rearing but with some deficiencies in support and/or working together.	Strong parental coalition; agreement and cooperation in child-rearing; sharing of pleasure and mutual support.
Parents support children and enjoy being with them but with minor or occasional problems in relating to the children.	Parents show care and concern; understand and pay attention to children appropriately; and are ready to participate in their activities.
Child--parent relationships are secure, but with mild difficulties in some areas or between particular dyads.	Children relate to both parents; are cooperative yet spontaneous; feel safe and show appropriate dependence.
Siblings affiliate with some limited rivalry, quarrelling, or lack of contact.	Siblings interact freely with shared enjoyment, affection, concern; differences can be resolved.

1. The grandmother gives Hava to her mother to play with. Mother lifts Hava to her face; Hava cries; mother looks startled and thrusts Hava in her grandmother's arms.
2. Whilst grandmother is asked her opinion about the cause of Hava's injuries, she suddenly decides Hava is hungry and starts bottle-feeding her.
3. Grandmother gives Hava to her mother to feed. She puts her into a small chair and mother roughly thrusts the bottle into Hava's mouth; Hava cries. Grandmother takes over the feed.

Concrete items of this nature alert the clinician, but they need to be built up into more coherent and meaningful episodes.

The second case is one of sexual abuse. The therapist met the family—father, mother, and 12-year-old Tina—after the diagnosis of sexual abuse had been made. Tina had spoken to a friend at school, who spoke to a teacher, who reported it to the Social Services department, who then investigated the case with the police. Tina was able to describe her abuse by her father, which had extended over a period of two years or more and had included attempted intercourse. Her father had immediately accepted responsibility for the abuse.

Both parents came from Italy and had met in this country, and Tina was their only child. The father was living in a probation hostel awaiting trial; Tina was living with her mother. The family therapist met first with Tina, then the father and mother, with Tina's agreement. The therapist also met together with the social worker concerned with Tina and her mother, and the probation officer who was to make a report on the father to the court when he was to receive sentence. The aim of this network session was to bring the family together for the first time so that the father could take responsibility for the abuse and a process of assessment and therapy work could begin.

The family found their own positions, and Tina seated herself between her parents; the therapist and professionals seated to complete a circle. A particular set of items of conversation and action emerged during the therapist's exploration of the father's responsibility.

Therapist: Why were you put in
   prison?

Mr M: I assaulted my daughter
   and there was incest.

*This is an unusual response: to
use the language of assault and
incest is quite rare.*

[Mother puts her arm out to
comfort Tina, but she shakes it
off.]

First item of note.

Therapist: How old was Tina
   when you started to assault
   her?

Mr M: She was twelve.

Therapist: Where was your wife
   when these assaults
   happened?

Mr M: She was at home. Tina
   wasn't feeling well—she had
   back trouble, she asked me to
   put cream on her back.

Therapist: That's how it
   started? Do you think when
   Tina asked you to put cream
   on her back she wanted you
   to be sexual with her?

Mr M: No, it just happened.

*This is a far more frequent re-
sponse from Mr M, as if the
event had had no pre-medita-
tion, occurred out of the blue, a
way of de-constructing responsibility, and a story that released
him from some idea of being
aroused by his daughter.*

Therapist: How do you feel
   about what you did to your
   daughter?

Mr. M: Ashamed. I have nothing against her. I blame myself. I'm sorry, I'm so ashamed. I would like to explain to her.

An interesting response, as if he is struggling with a construction that *she is* to blame!

Therapist: Is there something you could say to Tina about how you feel—could you say something simple (inviting him to talk directly to her) and perhaps begin the process of creating a more functional alternative story for Tina?

Mr M (to therapist): May I ask her forgiveness?

Therapist: Why don't you talk to her?

[At this point Mr. M touches the upper part of Tina's leg and immediately touches her shoulder]

Second item of note.

Mr M: Can I ask your forgiveness?

[He starts crying, and buries his head in his hands, sobbing]

Third item of note.

Therapist: It's okay to cry about painful things.

[Tina puts out her hand and gives a comforting gesture on his arm]

Fourth item of note

[Mr M goes on sobbing noisily; Mrs M takes out a hankie and uses it to dab her own eyes]

Fifth item of note.

Therapist: It's very special that father can ask you to forgive

| him, but (to Mr M) I'd like you to control yourself. I don't want Tina to be any more upset by you than she is. | The therapist, sensing a further victimization of Tina, by her father crying, and the impossible demand to be forgiven, gets the situation under control to prevent an alternative story emerging of the father as the despairing victim. |

These *items* all have a sense of clinical meaning and arise from the context of the interview. But without being put into context fully, they do not have coherence or a fuller clinical meaning and could be described as "ordinary" responses to the matters being discussed.

To helpfully describe such families we need to move up a level to describe the above series of items as an episode of interaction, and commonly an episode is given coherence through the behavioural responses that qualify the verbal statement.

Level 3—Episodes of interaction

Descriptions at this level provide a first contextual organization of both concepts and items into episodes that involve the whole family and, obviously, the therapist and other professionals involved.

An episode is an actual combination which has an inherent completeness and a coherence in time. The inquiring system is *synthetic*; facts, behaviours, and ideas are seen as inevitably interacting, each shaping and explaining the other and so producing an inherent ambiguity of description.

Because the demarcation and punctuation of episodes is based on pre-existing ideas and conceptions, different ways of describing the same thing are possible. It is possible to bring together the items described above into an episode, or sequence, and link this to the realities of family life, in a way that descriptions at lower levels do not.

The items described above can be described as a sequence. What sort of episodes do the items described in Hava's family suggest? Grandmother is clearly wanting to demonstrate her daughter's competence—giving Hava to her to play with or feed—yet each time either Hava gets distressed and triggers an aversive response on mother's part, or mother demonstrates an aversive feeding and handling response, grandmother takes over. The grandmother, when faced with the issue of the abuse, responds by perceiving a non-existent need to feed Hava. Such episodes, if repeated on a number of occasions in a microcosm, create and re-create the trauma-organized system—aversive, rejecting behaviour by the mother to the baby, the baby's traumatized aversive response, the grandmother rescuing and "over-responding" to her daughter and grandaughter's needs, maintaining the system.

When the reality of Tina's abuse by her father is confronted, Tina at first rejects her mother's attempt to comfort her. Father appears sad and guilty, yet he asserts his closeness to his daughter during his attempt to gain forgiveness by touching her in an inappropriate way at first, e.g. touching Tina's thigh, then her arm. His extreme distress triggers an attempt on her part to comfort him; he comforts himself, the mother comforts herself, and Tina is left isolated in the context of the various professionals who represent social realities as far as his abusive action and failure of care is concerned—again a microcosm of actions representing victimizing and victim action in the family context of the trauma-organized system.

The family and professionals have allowed a situation to develop where inappropriate contact occurred—e.g. the daughter sat between her parents, close to her father—rather than insisting on a more appropriate seating arrangement for a first meeting.

The emotional distance between the mother and daughter is emphasized with failure to comfort; an intense closeness between father and daughter is revealed; and a mutual comforting response on her part is brought forth and his sobbing induced a sympathetic response in the professional network with him as the victim, leaving his daughter isolated until the therapist takes control.

As clinicians we feel the urge to put such episodes in the context of other episodes we have observed, we need to hear about the family's and other professionals' observations and accounts of their lives. We need to contextualize such observations, through exploration of personal and family historical and social contexts to move up one more level in the framework to Level 4, Patterns of meanings.

Level 4—Patterns of meaning

Level 4 descriptions produce *patterns of meaning* by placing family episodes such as the one described above into context. Episodes can be reflexively placed into their own context, and, of course, we are concerned about episodes that regularly repeat the cycle—they feed back on themselves, occur without provocation, and become a primary preoccupation in family life.

When exploring the connections in Hava's family, we learnt that Hava's mother was adopted, her parents being unable to have their own children. She was described as a very easy child, spoiled and indulged, and "perfect" apart from "tantrums" which occurred in her adolescence. Hava was also described as being a perfect baby, until the age of three months when she started to have "colic". Hava's mother felt overwhelmed and desperately looked for help and support. She could not cope with Hava's crying, feeding went poorly, she failed to thrive for a time, was injured—without explanation—and grandmother took over her care. Hava is once more indulged, fed on the dot whether hungry or not, is once more seen as perfect; but each time her mother tries to handle her it goes wrong, there is mutual aversion between mother and baby, and grandmother rescues.

There are of course some deeper meanings and "unspoken" stories, feared disasters, which are only revealed through observation, e.g. the "fears" of the mother who adopts of rejection, which creates the over-feeding indulgence of the grandmother, the explosive response of the "over-controlled" child—Hava's mother—and the recreation of these explosions when she is frustrated by the baby's crying. In other words, the familiar failure to develop alternative coping strategies with limited resources.

Frequently such stories and meanings are co-created through imaginative leaps and speculations on the therapist's part. This leads to the search for meanings and stories co-created during the assessment process.

The episode above in the M family—isolation between mother and child, protective and emotional closeness between father and daughter, the victimizing stance of the abuser, the traumatic-victim response of Tina, and distance between father and mother—may have characterized the period before abuse was revealed, or it may be a post-disclosure pattern following the separation of the father, and his intense distress-triggering sympathetic response.

The session continued with an attempt by the professionals and family to explore the meaning issues.

Therapist (to Mrs M): When we spoke to you, you gave us to understand that Mr M had already told you how ashamed he was when you saw him in prison.

Mrs M: Yes, that's correct

Therapist: Do you think your husband understands the effect of his abuse on Tina?

Mrs M: Yes—he knows she will never forget. None of us will ever forget—we've always been a close family; we've all suffered a lot.

Mrs M is indicating a forceful protective stance towards her daughter. She has supported her throughout. It is interesting to note her passivity in the face of the previous powerful response and Tina's rejections of her earlier.

Therapist: Have you talked together to understand why your husband turned to Tina in a sexual way—to have sex with her?

Mrs M: We've tried, there wasn't much time to talk—10 minutes sometimes in prison.

Therapist (turning to Probation Officer): You've met with Mr M?

Probation Officer: We have had three meetings. One thing he described was pressure from his own mother. Their marriage was met with disapproval. His mother

This may be a distraction, but issues "on the top" of people's agenda may be important in formulating meanings and stories that connect with abusive actions.

hoped to arrange a marriage for him. But he chose Mrs M and the marriage was difficult.

Therapist: How is this connected with Mrs M's abuse?

Probation Officer: There is no connection yet.

Mrs M (breaks in, showing a degree of force): This is where the trouble started, she came to visit and gave us a lot of trouble, she was horrible to all three of us; whatever we said was no good!

Confirms and describes the stress the family was living under, a generic aspect in abuse of many varieties, and the long-standing disapproval and scape-goating of Mr M by his mother—emotional abuse extending to his whole family, as an aspect of their general sense of victimiza-tion.

Therapist: How was your relationship during the abuse?

Mrs M: We never had any problems during the abuse. She (indicating the social worker) wanted us to separate—but we were alright—no arguments—rows.

She is indicating the familiar coming together of the par-ents—against Social Services—no problems.

Therapist: Any stresses or pressures on you?

[Both parents look down]

Mr M: We were both sad when we found we could not have any more children. After

Mr M takes the lead. The issue of infertility he raises has obvious links with his sexual actions

Tina was born we decided not to have more children; we had a house to buy, a mortgage. When we paid it off, we decided to try for children. We tried for about three years without success. We went to the hospital for checks—both of us.

with his daughter—both as justification and as a rationalization and perhaps a connection with the general disapproval of his wife and himself by his mother.

Therapist: Did they find anything?

Mrs M: It was me. I did not produce enough eggs. I went for artificial insemination—it didn't work.

Mrs M taking responsibility on herself!

Mr M: I don't want to say in front of Tina.

A strange comment given his abusive actions.

Therapist: It's okay to say.

Mr M: I wasn't strong enough to.

Therapist: Not strong enough from your side?

An important meaning in terms of infertility, powerlessness, and the connections with the paternal grandmother's critical belittling approach.

Therapist: Which of the two of you feels most sad that there was a failure?

Mrs M: It is me.

Therapist (to Mr M): Do you agree your wife most feels she's failed—how did you know your wife's feelings?

Therapist picks up the sense of failure taken on by the mother which may be an "internal" conversation justifying his abuse of Tina—the second wife!

Mr M: She was not happy—as we went to bed she turned aside.

Meanings given to a reality and alternative story may often be found in the opposites which constitute many conversations. There is no pre-defined limit to the meanings and stresses linked to the episode and conversation described. Other episodes, information, enlarge meanings; deeper and more complex meanings emerge; more comprehensive stories to account for the perceptions and experiences develop. All perspectives need to be brought to bear to bring out the fullest possible meaning of any actual episode. The episode could be reframed in many different ways, and a variety of different alternative stories may be developed.

(1) The girl's protection of the father—putting her arm on his to comfort him, remaining silent for so long—could be connoted as an attempt to maintain a story of family togetherness, a fear of her parents separation, an attempt to avoid her own sense of outrage or proving grandmother right. The father's attention to his daughter may be connoted as a misplaced and inappropriate way of protecting his wife, because of their growing awareness that their own sexual relationship was not producing the further babies that she longed for. The mother's distancing from her daughter may be connoted as an expression of her anger at her daughter displacing her, or as protecting her husband from having to be aware of his role in the infertility which they were facing.

(2) The father's self-pitying, begging for forgiveness, evoking his daughter's protective response, may be seen as a way of maintaining his position of power and authority in the family through "weakness", despite his abusive action. The story of his sorrow and guilt may undermine understandable outrage. The rejection of mother by the daughter is an aspect of a story created by father, to reinforce her feeling of rejection and uselessness in the context of his interest in the daughter. The father's response of self-abasement towards the professionals could be seen as a story that brings forth a desire to be helpful on the parts of agents of society, rather than to evoke a condemning, blaming, punitive approach.

(3) By bringing information from conversations about father's history, a meaning and story emerges of his own sense of powerlessness in relation to his own mother's abuse and rejection of him, as the origin of the father's abusive cycle. He therefore emerged from childhood with no language for the emotional closeness he

was likely to discover in adolescence, together with sexuality. He rapidly left Italy to create a "new" story, he met his wife and married her in defiance of his mother, yet his grievance with his mother continues to be echoed by the family.

His own response to powerlessness—to be powerful, to want to take revenge on his mother—created a "critical story" which constantly lived with him and from which he or his family could not escape. Tina is their princess, the child who has to have everything and be everything that the father did not have. She is a source of idealization and yet also of envy, of love, and also of resentment. Sexualization of the closeness represents an action to feel powerful, to create the baby he could not create with his wife, and yet to attack and divert himself of his own privation and loss.

Inevitably, once his abusive behaviour is initiated it develops its own addictive, reflexive demand fueled by his perceptions of Tina's response—silence—as "agreement".

(4) The mother had a loving relationship with her own parents, yet was preoccupied with her sister's childlessness. She created a story of also being childless herself and so immediately became pregnant when she and her husband married. She, too, idealizes Tina and wants more children, but puts off the pregnancy to build a home. Later both parents prove to be sub-fertile. For her, awareness of the abuse leads to retreat, helplessness, and hopelessness. She tries to respond to her daughter, but retreats and so the over-close contact with father is not contested.

(5) Using another set of meanings it is possible to see father and Tina creating the story of a marital pair, asserting their caring and sexual relationship, as organized by the father, whilst the mother is seen as the rejected child both by father and by the daughter he has organized.

Such frameworks are not mutually exclusive, and the deeper the therapeutic work itself continues, the more complex the conversations. A variety of different contexts are necessary for such conversations to develop alternative stories, e.g. family meetings, groups for Tina and her peers, groups for mother and other mothers in the same situation, groups for father and other men in the same situation. All such contacts deepen the meanings, increase the complexity of conversation about such relationships, and ensure the emergence of a more functional set of meanings and alternative stories towards protectiveness and care rather than use and abuse.

Inevitably, particularly in the early phases of treatment, it is essential to provide a single complete story account of the family as it is now. The therapist needs to co-create and synthesize a model of the family, using all the descriptions so far obtained. This leads to the next level.

Level 5—Holistic formulation

Level 5 is a *holistic formulation* where the therapist provides a *single complete* narrative of the family as it is now. This integrates those aspects of the family described at lower levels into an account of the family as a whole. This is a truly systemic description and narrative of the family, since it integrates all lower level descriptions, and should take all relevant factors into account in generating a model of how the family works which can be used for intervention. We have described (Bentovim & Kinston, 1991) the full implications of such an approach, the instruments that are required to record information, and the different ways of helping families and individuals towards providing sufficient information to be able to make a holistic formulation.

A particular approach to making a holistic formulation is the creation of a *focal* hypothesis which focuses on the specific effects of traumatic events and stressful relationships on the functioning of individuals and the family as a whole. The following questions have to be answered:

1. *How can violent or abusive acts be restated in an interactional form?* How can violence be connected to the family's way of being, and vice versa, and how do professionals respond, and how does the family respond to professionals?

2. *What is the function of the current interaction?* How would the family interact if there were no child or parent to abuse, or if the professionals failed to intervene?

3. *What are the feared disasters and anxieties in the family?* What is it that is feared would happen if events were addressed and spoken about?

4. *What is the link to original stressful experiences?*   Which past experiences in the family of origin or the current family are judged to be linked to the present family abusive interaction patterns?

In the Hava's family the process could be represented through the following stages:

1. We can see the mother's abusive acts as an attack on the baby who should be "perfect", and yet who cries and will not eat, will not grow. This leads to the baby being given to the grandmother to care for, which she does in an "over-responsive" fashion. Professionals are blamed for not helping, abuse is denied, and the family is described as perfect.

2. Without the child to abuse, major issues over the "separation" struggle between the adolescent mother and grandmother would have to be faced, e.g. the struggle between expected perfect compliance and angry independence.

3. Acknowledgement by any family member of "abusive action" rather than being perfect, might imply a "permanent" separation, as it would reveal the mother and the grandmother's incompetent parenting and the connection with explosive responses.

4. The original stressful events seem to focus on the original childlessness of the maternal grandmother and her response to it.

In summary, the narrative could be simplified to "Childrens' frustrations can be filled by perfect parenting. The child who fails to be perfect deserves to be blamed and punished."
In the M family the narrative could be represented as follows:

1. Mr M's arousal and abusive activity can be seen as a way of asserting potency in the context of infertility, asserting closeness through the familiar role of sexuality, divesting himself of humiliation by attacking his "princess" daughter, excluding mother.

2. Without a child to abuse, it is likely that there would be mutual antagonism and criticism between the parents, linked to infertility.

3. The disaster would be the justification of the grandmother's condemnation of the marriage and a sense of failure and power-lessness.

4. The original stressful experiences are the father's long-standing emotional abuse and criticisms by his own mother, and the mother's family childlessness.

In summary, the "focal" hypothesis can be stated as: "Powerless-ness, humiliation, and childlessness are avoided by a 'secret' addictive abuse of the 'princess' child, whose silence in the face of threats maintains family togetherness in the face of a critical grand-parent."

Disclosure seemed to be precipitated for Tina by the balance of keeping the secret being exceeded by her personal sense of trauma-tization—flashbacks, feeling overwhelmed, and fears of pregnancy. Disclosure led to what appeared to be a very different system—guilt, distress, self-abasement—instead of threat and control. It can be hypothesized that self-abasement could be a way of arousing professional and family compassion. For the father, contact was maintained with his daughter in a "care-taking role" towards him, yet a distance was maintained between himself and his wife, and his wife and daughter. A similar "family" togetherness is main-tained. There is, however, the beginning of a real awareness of trau-matizing behaviour and its effects.

Level 6—Type formulation

Level 6 refers to the typing or categorization of a whole family based on one or more of its features that are held to be characteris-tic. This level of narrative is appropriately regarded as higher since it should by definition encompass and put into perspective all nar-ratives and descriptions at a lower level and places the family under consideration in the wider context of all families.

Such a notion requires substantial validation to be helpful. Certain entities, such as the *"psychosomatic family"* introduced by Minuchin, have been subject to scrutiny and have been found to cover a proportion of families seen. The issue of whether the "violent" or "victimizing" family is an appropriate category or not, has been a subject of controversy. The notion of families "liable to abuse" has been described, through characteristic description—young, single, vulnerable parents, lower social class, stressed like Hava's parents. But as was demonstrated earlier, the differences are often subtle, and attempts to sort out "at risk" parents at birth has not been successful.

There have also been descriptions, for instance, of the "incestuous family", implying that characteristics of the participants produce a particular family context associated with high degrees of secrecy, and with the development of sexual relationships across generation boundaries as ways of avoiding conflict between parents, or as ways that a family has to regulate the conflict within it to measurable levels. To some extent the M family could be seen to reflect some of these characteristics.

There has, however, been a vigorous attack on such approaches on the grounds that sexual abuse is frequently only known to the victimizer and victim, not to other family members. It is also argued that the notion of an "incestuous family" fits into the constructions that professionals have about them, rather than fitting the families themselves. Sexual abuse often occurs as a direct result of the action of a man with an abusive orientation towards children, who literally grooms a particular child to respond to him and manages the whole family situation in such a way that secrecy, and a sense of guilt and responsibility, is felt by the child and/or by the mother which maintains the power and authority of the abuser, again as could be seen in the M family.

The notion of a *trauma-organized system* is an attempt to get away from a polarity between the "system" creating the problem, or the "individual" creating the system. It argues that events in the lives of individuals create the context for the stories by which members live their lives, the relationships they make, the abusive actions that they initiate, and their responses to those actions. So it is not either the individual creating the system, or the system the individual, but both—a transactional process involving the individual and the family in a particular societal context.

Trauma-organized systems require a *cultural context*, e.g. for the M family from Italy where fertility and large families are valued, and where authority is given to men and to the grandparental generation. Patriarchal views re men, women, and children are common contexts for trauma-organized systems.

The *family context* contains family-of-origin stresses, e.g. the "scape-goated" role of the child that Mr M, as surrogate for his father, suffered through rejection, contempt, and poor care: a child is abused rather than a partner confronted.

His solution was to act—to leave Italy, to marry a woman who had fears that she would not conceive. The child resulting was idealized, given everything, and seen as everything father and mother wished for.

The issue of infertility is the sort of *recent stress* that the familiar "solution" of action does not encompass. It can only be overcome by *doing* things. Frustration and powerlessness become transformed into a desire for action. The couple blame each other, yet this will confirm the grandmother's condemnation of their choice. A familiar pattern of sexualization, of intimacy, common in rejected boys, occurs instead. As Tina innocently asks her father to put some cream on her back which is sore, a sexual impulse is triggered, he touches her breast, and the addictive abusive cycle is initiated recreating the abusive script.

Categorization of traumatic handling after disclosure

The "style" of dealing with traumatic events may dictate the sort of family life that develops, which could include the way problems develop. It is possible to see a number of different stories emerging that represent ways in which trauma and a traumatic event is handled by the family, after disclosure of abuse for instance. The most positive form of handling is where the members of the family are beginning to acknowledge, and can at least face the reality of, the abuse, with the appropriate abuser taking responsibility, the child being basically protected as in the M family and being allowed to think about and co-create an alternative truer story of her abusive experience rather than maintain silence, deletion, and a "hole" in the mind.

The reverse of this is total denial—no abuse has occurred, there is an absolute blanket of silence, and a wall is built around the family, abuse is never spoken about. It is the construction of the professionals and not of the family. Hava's family showed these characteristics. They had no meaningful comprehensive story to account for, recognize, and confront abusive action. The response to a request for an explanation is silence, a minimum statement—she must have hit her head on the side of the cot; the dog bumped into mother whilst feeding her; feeding was perfect; she could not possibly be losing weight, or not growing. Yet the paediatrician's story was that the fracture sustained could only be the result of a ten-foot fall onto concrete, or a hard blow to the head. Thus the stories of the family and of the professionals reflect entirely different scripts: the "perfect" parent, the professionals, the "dangerous" parent. There was a real failure to co-create a story between the professionals and the family to account for the abuse.

Another pattern is to construct a story that blames X as the source of all problems, so that perhaps father and mother will come together to construe the child as totally bad, to blame, as having a totally malign influence. There are no attempts to understand factors that have played a part, there is no dialogue or construction of any narrative to make sense of experiences except in terms of badness. The child may persistently be seen as seductive, as deserving punishment. Alternatively, as in the T family, the mother might see herself as the source of all problems—she did not satisfy her husband, she was a poor wife, a poor partner.

Level 7—Requisite formulation

Dealing with family violence and abuse requires the therapist to contemplate how this family might function if therapeutic work was successful—an "idealistic" narrative of how the family might be. This approach is more essential in dealing with family violence than with other problems presenting to clinicians. By definition, the therapist is always working with protection agencies who may have a "parental role". This ethical position is different when the "state" is the parent in comparison to the family having control of the situation.

It is possible to be "neutral" about the results of therapy and what is to be achieved for a family seeking help on its own behalf. Obviously the therapist has to be generally "helpful", but the "power" of being able to reframe and connote apparently pathological behaviour as helpful gives a flexibility to the therapist's position which is less available when family violence has occurred. Where family violence has occurred the "victimizer/victim" process may well have resulted in a situation where neutrality is "impossible" by definition. A protective agency needs to be involved; there may be separation of a child, or a partner in a refuge. The therapist's role is not to be neutral to family events, but to be able to engage with the family to assess future possibilities. A future that contemplates victimization cannot be accepted for the victim. Victim or abusive behaviour cannot be positively connoted; the critical issue is the context for reversal of these dangerous patterns.

The "requisite" description has to take into account the "potential" for co-creating stories and realities. For each individual or family sub-system—partners, parents, parent–child, child(ren)—can a safe context be created, can abusing actions be reversed? To answer these questions it requires information from the family, from research, and from the therapeutic contexts available.

In the M family, there is a hopeful aspect of their presentation: the possibility of co-creating the story of their actions. It becomes possible to think of helping the girl to become assertive and develop a positive image and story for herself to reverse traumatic effects. Group work with contemporaries helps overcome the sense of powerlessness, and previous difficulties in self-protection, to develop a "strong" self-image to prevent future abuse.

Mr M could qualify to participate in a group for men who have also abused, to help define his actions more clearly. He can discover, through the conversation which he and other men who abuse have, about his cycle of arousal, excitement, fear, and the way these organized his actions. He can confront his omnipotent story that he would never be discovered, and could explore the excitement which maintains itself. He can make a contract to discover if he can find a truly safe parent within him to combat his abusive, victimizing self.

The mother needs be able to express her own grievances, her own disappointments, a story to resolve the pull between a need to be a partner and to be a parent. Family network meetings are needed to strengthen the tie between mother and daughter and help to reestablish appropriate distance and appropriate rules for living.

Tasks of professionals and therapists thus emerge from a consideration of what goals need to be achieved, and the different modalities and ways of creating the ideal outcome.

We found it far more difficult to find a "future" satisfactory story for Hava and her family. The discrepancy between their actions and their story was so great that it was difficult to contemplate a safe situation for Hava between her grandparents and parents. Their reiterated story of the perfect family created an impenetrable barrier for professional action. It may well be that a contract of work was necessary to test their capacity to develop and co-create a more satisfactory explanation and comprehensive story to envisage a safe future for Hava and her family.

CHAPTER EIGHT

Treating
the trauma-organized system

ASSESSMENT FOR TREATMENT

A fundamental characteristic of the treatment of trauma-organized systems is the tremendous difficulty in breaking the taboo of silence and, once the taboo is broken, to maintain and develop the resulting conversations for the victim, the victimizer, and other protective figures in the family. There is a tendency for disclosures to be disqualified, to disappear in a flurry of denial and blaming.

The first step of treatment is to explore the extent of violent action within the family context, to ensure that a victim is protected, and that through breaking the taboo of silence there can be an open acknowledgement by family members of what has happened within the family situation, what factors have initiated abusive action, and what factors are maintaining it.

In this first phase one of the major decisions to be taken is how best to ensure the protection of a child—or an adult—victim of abuse. Is there a natural protector within the family, e.g. can a non-abusive parent understand and believe sufficiently to be able to protect against further abusive action? Does the abuser take sufficient responsibility for his or her action to enable appropriate statutory services to work with families on a voluntary basis? Is there a need for appropriate statutory action excluding an abusive partner or parent from the home, or does a child have to be removed for his or her own safety?

Whilst the taboo of secrecy is being challenged, therapists cannot work alone since therapeutic agencies by definition do not have the statutory authority to be able to take the sort of action that will ensure a child's protection. It is essential that there be a link between the therapeutic agency and the statutory agency with sufficient authority to ensure that action can be taken on behalf of the victim or a perpetrator.

To assess these issues requires the combination of family and individual interviews. A child living in an abusive atmosphere will not speak about his or her experiences in the presence of a family member who is part of that system. Even though a non-abusive parent can often be of assistance to a child in beginning to share his or her experiences, that parent may unwittingly be part of the trauma-organized system. Thus despite themselves they may give the child a cue which may be silencing, in the way that Mrs T did in the family session (chapter six). The partner subject to intimidation and abuse cannot trust an abusive partner not to become aggrieved and punitive when revealing the extent of abusive interaction. Externalizing techniques are often necessary to help the traumatized victim begin to share experiences rather than continue to be organized into silence.

There are a number of areas that need to be explored to help decide which family member can be helped, where the victimized member needs to live, and what the longer term prospects are, e.g. for rehabilitation of a child to a seriously abusive family, or for a partnership to have some prospect of stable outcome.

Responsibility for the abuse

The first key issue when confronted with a failure to provide adequate care or with serious abuse is how much responsibility the individual takes for the state of the child, or partner where this is relevant. How aware are such individuals that they need to change, and make some major shift in their behaviour or relationship, to ensure the future safety and protection of a child or partner?

In the cases I have already discussed, Mr M, although he attempts to win the professionals' good opinion, does take full responsibility immediately for what his daughter stated. Carl J, however (chapter four), absolutely refused to accept any responsibility for the statement that his stepdaughter made about his abusive action. Indeed, when his wife attempted to bring the issues up he reminded her that she had said that she would only believe it if she saw it with her own eyes. Hava and her family could offer no satisfactory explanation for her abuse.

Ali, the man who had abused his partner Carmel so horrendously (chapter four), initially claimed that it was a form of sexual bondage which his partner had wanted. When seen at a later date he displayed a considerable sense of shame and self-disgust at his action. Other men may indicate that, despite their partner suffering a variety of injuries, they had only ever hit their partner by mistake on one occasion, provoked by them, absolutely denying the quite clear evidence of frequent injuries.

Jamie's mother (chapter five) indicated at first quite forcefully, "I have not injured my son", therefore implying that it was her husband who was maintaining a denial. Such was the concern about the baby's injuries that the child was removed, and at a later date rehabilitated to the mother who was unable to take real responsibility for her son's injuries for a year or two. Thus denial of responsibility is a frequent aspect of trauma-organized systems, and the need to confront this issue protectively is very great. How can somebody who is unaware of their actions ever be trusted not to act again if the same context should arise in the future?

An extension of the issue of responsibility for direct abusive action is the attitude of the other parent in child abuse. Carl J's wife (chapter four) was torn between believing her daughter and being organized into her husband's belief. Often the trauma-organized system means that not only is a child abused, but a partner is intimidated or threatened into the dominating story. Lorraine's mother (chapter four), after she had been able to name her father as an abuser when caring for her, began systematically to threaten, bully, and tell her to change her story. It was then revealed that both her parents had in fact abused her. To take another example, a parent might frequently telephone a child in care saying that unless she changes her story the father will commit suicide, or that he cannot tolerate life without a partner.

It is very difficult to be certain of a "protective" parent maintaining a caring stance in the face of the pressure of her own needs, or from a powerful partner. The wife of a man confronted with the probability that he administered noxious substances to a child, which resulted in serious eye inflammation, indicated that she felt that her children would find good homes, and good caretakers, but she would never find a partner such as her husband. When asked if she had to make a choice what she would do, she indicated, to her husband's surprise, that she would choose him rather than the child.

In spouse abuse, e.g. Ali and Carmel, despite physical violence, intimidation, attack, and belittlement, the hope for a magical redemption of the relationship may be held out as a way to overcome and delete abusive experiences.

The ability to put the needs of the victim first

The second major issue is the ability of family members to put the needs of the victim first, to show an appropriate degree of warmth versus an attitude that blames and scapegoats the child. Carl J's stepdaughter, for instance, was absolutely determined that she was not going to live with her stepfather, and because her mother could not separate herself from him, she lived separately from both. Her mother was both angry with her for living apart and, at times, sympathetic. The stepfather was contemptuous and dismissive of her because she could not speak across the video link.

We saw with the M family that although the father was able to take responsibility, the trauma-organized process asserted a close relationship between the father and daughter but there was a distance between mother and daughter, with the mother comforting herself, not her daughter, during a period of distress in the session. There would need to be further exploration to know whether there was a genuine warmth which could be brought out between mother and daughter, to answer the question of whether there was sufficient care and concern to believe that the child could remain with the mother.

In partner abuse, the issue of the extended family response may be an important aspect of whether a victim of marital abuse can find protection and support from an extended family, or will be criticized, blamed, and almost driven back into the arms of the abusive partner who shows contrition, shame, and guilt.

Recognition of the need for help
for long-standing problems

The third issue is the degree of recognition on the part of the victimizer that he or she has a need for help for long-standing personal, marital, or relationship problems, for drug or alcohol abuse, or for psychiatric illness, versus a denial that such problems are present or a gross minimization of their severity and relevance. If the individual victimizer is taking little or no responsibility for the abuse, he or she will be unlikely to acknowledge the presence of personal factors that may, in addition, play a major role in violent or abusive actions.

Mr M was able to give a coherent account, with the help of a probation officer who knew him, about his long-standing grievances with his controlling mother, the recent marital stresses that had accompanied the investigations, and the failure of further conceptions; a link with his own childhood rejection and emotional abuse could then be established.

Such investigations are an essential part of making assessments of perpetrators for their degree of dangerousness.

A 15½-year-old youngster who was living in a community for learning-disordered young people presented an extremely worrying picture when he described his intense overwhelming rape fantasies and the way these were connected with a long-standing grievance towards his mother and grandmother who had abused him.

Such issues as long-standing alcoholic problems may only come to light when, for instance, a family attends a day or residential centre and the extensiveness of individual and inter-personal problems are revealed. The G family was referred following a death of a child which had occurred whilst the father in the family was in prison. The death has been caused by a co-habitee, who had shaken and battered the baby. The issue for the father was his feeling that there would be no future for them as a family if it appeared that his wife was at all implicated in the abuse of this baby.

The wife, on the other hand, confronted her husband with the fact that it was his criminality—his habitual thieving—that led to him being away from the family and therefore making her vulnerable and alone. Only over time was it realized that the father was drinking heavily each day and, indeed, that a long-standing alcohol problem was one of the factors that led to his criminal activities. He indicated an awareness that a court would consider that an alcoholic problem would make for future instability in the family. He acknowledged that the court would want him to be dry for at least six months before feeling he could be trusted. He went into an alcohol unit but came out within a week and then turned up provocatively drunk to sessions. In a sense he was making a strong statement about his capacities to support his wife and their children, and this could be connoted as his way of indicating that he did not have the resources to change the trauma-organized system that he, his wife, and his children were caught up in. The notion of a therapeutic trial to assess whether parents are able to acknowledge and begin to reverse such long-standing problems may be a helpful approach to the assessment of treatability during the early stages following recognition of severe family-violence patterns.

Such assessments need to be multi-modal, looking at individual, parental, and family functioning: the use of day and residential settings where families can attend are very helpful in finding out whether trauma-organized systems are modifiable or whether they have such a hold on individuals that, for instance, children must be removed. The longer-term follow-up for seriously abused children rehabilitated to their own families indicates the very high risk of recurrent physical and emotional abuse. Review of a variety of research indicates a re-abuse rate of between 30 and 60%.

When Asen, George, Piper, and Stevens (1989) used an assessment period to decide whether rehabilitation was a possibility in serious abuse, they felt that 30% of such cases could not be rehabilitated. Follow-up of those other families where there appeared to be sufficient ground to continue work indicated a far lower incidence of abuse, perhaps as little as 3%. But the indications are that 30% of serious-abuse cases have trauma-organized systems of such severity that they cannot be resolved within the time-frame for the children. In our own series of severely sexually abused children, just over a third of mothers were unable to believe or develop a story that their children had been abused. Therefore, rehabilitation of children to those families could not be contemplated.

Potential for change observed

What is essential to observe over a period of assessment is whether parents can take responsibility not only in word, through development of an appropriate story, but also in deed, by demonstrating a different form of response to the child over a period of time. The major test is whether this change can occur within a child's time-frame. A particular stress for professionals is the situation when a parent, subjected to past and current violence, cannot develop an alternative story and way of being quickly enough to nurture the child.

In partner abuse, the issue is how much a man can, for instance, not only acknowledge the degree of abuse such as Ali was able to do, but also how much he is able to work with an agency to confront his abusive actions. During this period it may be helpful to have joint meetings with partners, as it is with families, to maintain the momentum of breaking the taboo about abusive action. However, it is unlikely that it would be possible to explore either the traumatic effects on the individual child or adult, or the extensiveness of abusive actions, abusive fantasies, or abusive cycles, whilst the partner is present. Goldner and her colleagues (1990) indicated that during their period of work with violent couples, there was a need for both individual and joint meetings.

In the assessment period in our Child Sexual Abuse Programme, there is a need for interviews with children alone, children with their protective parent, protective parents alone, the abuser alone, the abuser and partner, and the whole family context.

Although the family section of the T family assessment is described (chapter six) this was preceded by interviews with the children alone, with the mother alone, with the father alone, with the mother and children, and then with the father and children. Similarly, in the M family it was important during this phase to get to know Tina sufficiently to understand the extensiveness of her own abusive experience, the mother to help her think about the issues specifically for her as a parent and partner, and the father to help him confront the abusive cycle that he was caught in. Out of such assessments it becomes possible to see whether attachment patterns are rigidly fixed in aversive or highly ambivalent patterns, or there is a potential for change. The importance of one positive attachment model for a child has been revealed in the follow-up of individuals who have been abused during childhood; the importance of establishing whether there is a potential for such a positive attachment within the family, or whether it has to be sought outside, is an essential task during this assessment process.

Co-operation with professionals

To reverse trauma-organized systems requires the working together of a therapeutic agency and a protection agency. In the case of a child this needs to be the child-protection agency, and in spouse abuse it may well be the women's refuge which can lay down the rules for adequate and continuing protection. Although many families would like a therapeutic agency to be the only one they are in contact with, basically therapeutic agencies cannot protect anyone! Only a protection agency has the statutory power to take action and to empower the therapeutic agency to do the work necessary to achieve the reversal of traumatic effects.

In Hava's family, it was essential that the Social Services department had a parental authority for Hava's safety, although she was living with grandparents. In the M family, the court needs to give a probation officer the authority to plan where Mr M should live, and a social worker the authority to protect Tina.

The therapeutic agency can then ask Mr M what he feels would convince the probation and protection agency that it would be safe if he returned home. We can ask him how much understanding, how much detail he would have to share, how extensive the conversation would need to be, to reassure a protection agency that there could be a possibility of a safe return of Mr M to his family. How much work would we need to do with Tina, with her mother, to be able to say that Tina has fully got over her traumatic flash-backs and effects, and how long to know that her mother truly puts Tina's needs first.

One can say that as a therapeutic agency we may well have an instinctive trust of Mr M or Mrs M, but how can we as a professional agency possibly ask a protective agency or the court to make a decision based on our intuition, rather than on real thoroughgoing knowledge? How much work would Mr M feel would need to be done to achieve this goal? How would the court know that it would be safe? What would the court want for a child who may be in that court's or local authority's protection? For therapeutic agencies and family members to work together to convince the authority is a powerful tool to help achieve what is painful—talking about abusive experiences for the victim, talking about abusive actions for the victimizer, acknowledgement of what has happened by the parent who should have had a protective role. There can be an insistence on the need to develop an alternative model or story to relationships, to convince the court!

An important aspect of co-operativeness is the availability of therapeutic agencies, and of appropriate settings, for parents to be able to do the work to achieve change and to convince a court or protection agency. Insufficient residential and day settings are available, so it is essential that treatment agencies work closely with protection agencies to create a network of therapeutic settings where work can be done with families where violence occurs.

The role of group work for offenders, whether against children or partners, is an essential development, as is group work for children and for mothers and the use of family network approaches to bring together statutory agencies and therapeutic agencies to be able to assess safety and change. Protection work with children is now embedded in a complex structure of case conferences and a variety of statutory agencies with differing views about working together. Family members need therapeutic advocates who will undertake to do work even with serious abuse situations as an essential component of the whole structure.

ASSESSMENT OF ATTITUDES TO FAMILY VIOLENCE

When assessing treatability or potential for work, we have found it helpful to rate trauma-organized systems as hopeful, doubtful, or hopeless.

Hopeful situations

Hopeful situations are those where family members are able to acknowledge their role, or their responsibilities for the state of a child or partner. In such situations the victim is not excessively blamed but is seen as having been subject to an abusive act, and care is recognised as being essential. Other family members may need to recognise their own role in abuse and failure to care, even though they may not be directly responsible. Abusive individuals need to be willing to work on their problems and on the life experiences that may have had a role in bringing about the victimizer status. There needs to be appropriate agency support and a therapeutic plan with a sufficient degree of co-operativeness to feel that there is a good prospect of change. The M family was a good example of a "hopeful" situation.

In such cases it may well be possible to use voluntary agreements rather than having to use statutory instruments to achieve change.

If statutory means are essential because of the severity of abuse of a child or partner, then the courts need to indicate that a child cannot return unless individuals are willing to attend for appropriate therapeutic work. Professionals need to specify changes to be made and that there is a potential for work.

There is always a danger of compliance rather than genuine involvement in therapeutic work. Groups are helpful here, in that they provide a better model for a co-operative approach than individual work initially. For instance, a boy of 14 was willing to join a young offenders group because of what he stated were the *alleged* offences for which he was being made to take responsibility. At the third group meeting when other boys went round saying what offences they had been responsible for, he naturally and easily described his own abusive acts. Being confronted by others who employ the same deletions and denial of responsibility is a helpful way to begin facing abusive actions, and to develop a narrative that substitutes thought and a story rather than action.

Doubtful situations

Doubtful situations are those in which there is a degree of uncertainty as to whether victimizers are taking proper responsibility for the state of the victims. There may be a denial of the extent of the involvement, the victim may be attributed as having continuing responsibility for his or her own abuse, and there may be no revision of the original attribution. There may be a relative lack of support from other family members. The need of the partners for each other may be so great that the danger of re-abuse—which may then require a period of separation—cannot be confronted. There may be a limited perception for the need to change, and a discrepancy between the perceived needs of family members for help and their own willingness to acknowledge this.

Co-operativeness may be limited between parents and professionals, and there may be a considerable sense of doubt about commitment to change, even though resources are available to provide therapeutic input and maintain appropriate protection. It may well be that in these cases a variety of statutory instruments may be necessary to ensure protection, but almost inevitably in turn they may well arouse further anger and a bringing together of family members to minimize abusive interactions and to blame professionals.

Hopeless situations

These are situations where the degree of harm to the victim is totally denied, even when there is a professional consensus that violence has been committed. There may be a denial that abuse has occurred, professionals may be accused of putting the idea or story into a child or a partner's head, and the professionals who interviewed may be blamed. Other explanations and stories may be offered for fractures and bruising, and there may be a considerable coming together of family members, both nuclear and extended, to feel that the professionals are to blame, not the family members.

There may be a failure to acknowledge problems of alcoholism, psychiatric illness, long histories of violence, or major problems. Specific resources such as residential settings may be absent, or there may be insufficient taking of responsibility to make the use of such resources justifiable.

Typically, co-operation with professionals may have broken down, and there may be such stories of anger and grievance and feelings of being blamed and scape-goated that it is impossible to create the sort of alliance which leads to a sense of trust and makes protection possible. Full use of the statutory processes may be essential to protect a child in such family contexts. It is likely that there will be considerable battling over such issues, with recruiting of other professionals to create a massive trauma-organized system, to obliterate the traumatic actions within the family itself. Recruiting representatives in an adversarial court context for a father, a mother, a child, the local authority, the guardian of the child, even for a therapeutic agency, may complicate the most fiercely contended of cases.

THE ASSESSMENT PROCESS

To indicate the detailed process of such an assessment the G family are presented. The case to be described is one in a series used to validate the structure of the assessment model described here, that is, in terms of a degree of hopefulness, doubtfulness, or hopelessness.

Joanne Sylvester (1990) used an attributional framework to rate each of a series of cases in which I had assessed a degree of hopefulness, doubtfulness, and hopelessness. She then used the Leeds Attributional Coding System to look at the narrative that emerged and rate the attributions that family members had for the others' behaviour. The hypothesis to be tested was that in hopeful cases the parent would see herself or himself as responsible for what occurred to the children and that this would be reflected in those parents' narratives. That is, the parent would see himself or herself as the agent for negative or unhappy outcomes affecting the child.

In the more doubtful and hopeless cases it was expected that the children themselves would be seen as the cause, e.g. having brought abusive actions on to their own heads by their actions, rather than as attributable to something in the parents' actions. The theoretical basis for such an approach is that the *causes and reasons* parents offer for their childrens' behaviour are likely to influence the way parents feels about that behaviour, the meaning that parents give to it, and ultimately how they respond and how they are responded to. Thus such explanations tap into the continuing constructions and stories that parents and children have about themselves.

The research supported the basic structure of our assessment process in that in hopeful cases the parents were indeed more likely to continue to see themselves as the cause. In doubtful cases they were far more likely to see the child as having deserved punishment or abuse by their own actions. In hopeless cases there was more likelihood that parents would see themselves as the victims, would see actions very much directed towards themselves. They paid rather little attention to the child. This was not surprising because referrals were often made to us after a good deal of professional activity. It was not an uncommon response for parents to feel extremely persecuted and attacked by the system, particularly if they were resolutely unable to take responsibility for abusive actions, because of the processes they were caught up in.

Case example—The G family

A typical pattern which emerged was seen in Vanessa's family. She was a 13-year-old with spina bifida who had a disability both in appearance and in function and, as a result, had problems of mobility. She attended a normal school but complained she had few friends, and she was basically an unhappy child who described a punitive, angry atmosphere in her family. She had two non-handicapped older brothers. Initial interviews indicated that there was a good deal of anger evoked, and the father made very few statements in which he saw himself as responsible for negative outcomes that involved Vanessa. On the contrary, he made a great many statements that indicated that he saw his daughter as responsible. He felt himself to be the victim rather than the aggressor, even though, as in the extract to be reported, he described an incident where he had kicked her.

He felt himself the victim of her aggression and manipulation, far more than having any responsibility himself. On the other hand the pattern of responsibility described by the mother was quite different. Although she blamed her daughter, she also saw herself as the cause of the negative outcome or bad things occurring, far more than she blamed her daughter.

A classic pattern occurred of intense external blame on the father's part, and intense internal blame on the mother's part. The stage is set with Vanessa receiving entirely different messages, which inevitably has a binding and maintaining effect on the child. In the eyes of her father she can do no right, in the eyes of her mother she can do no wrong. She is thus triangled or bound into an impossible position. There is no possibility for her to do other than support her mother's view that she can do no wrong, whilst also confirming her father's view that she can do no right.

This is, of course, an extremely dangerous position. It is not surprising in the context of the assessment with both parents and Vanessa that a concern arose that severe injury could occur. Inevitably in a young person with a disability, issues of guilt and failure are aroused. Marital and parental disagreement are hidden by the focus on Vanessa.

Mother: On Thursday morning she howled the place down for this hairbrush, and I searched everywhere, I went into Timothy's room, Hugo's room, Vanessa's. I looked. I was running round like a dingbat whilst she roared the place down, really screaming. You (father) came down and you said if this nonsense doesn't stop immediately I'm going to thrash you. You went back upstairs, you went into the bathroom and started washing, and it continued. It went on for about three-quarters of an hour.

In this first statement by mother she is describing her response to Vanessa's howling the place down and indicating that her response to search everywhere," running like a dingbat" which reflects earlier statements that she had made indicating her own response to Vanessa's demand which was to try desperately to please her, reflecting her own self-blame for things that were wrong for Vanessa.

Father: And Hugo had an exam that day you know, and she knew this. This is the point, if she knows anything is going to happen she will

Father's response is to make an absolutely negative attribution view about her action, her deliberately disrupting the the household, planning, enjoying it, there deliberately disrupt the household. I mean you can see it happening . . . she plans it and she enjoys it, there's no question about it.

Therapist: What had happened to your brush that day?

Vanessa: I'm not saying anything.

Therapist: Well who had taken it in fact?

Father: She had, she hides it.

Mother: I can tell you, in the end of the day Vanessa did get a smack and she got a black eye with it.

Vanessa: I didn't get a smack, I got a kick in the face mum.

Father: Well she was on the floor and this had been going on for half an hour. I mean I don't keep records of these things, but you have to understand that this is not just one morning, but a whole series, getting near the point where it's near to murder. And that's quite where we are now. And if she had carried on with it, I probably would have murdered her. You have to understand that, I'm not kidding with these things.

being no question about it which indicates the complete conviction of his views and their stability and firmness of meaning.

Vanessa responds by describing exactly what happened, the fact that she got kicked.

Father with a great deal of difficulty acknowledges this and gives an indication of the script he writes for her.

When confronted with the demand to say exactly what happened—the need to be quite explicit and concrete about what occurred—he again makes a statement which repeats his basic attribution to her—"this is not just one morning, but a whole series, getting near the point where it's near to murder", and then going on to indicate the dangerousness, that he could have gone on to murder her.

Mother: I was trying to say to Carl (father) you know, keep calm, because Carl never comes down stairs in the morning. He came down twice and on the third occasion he came down and he bashed them, and he also bashed Hugo because he said well Hugo or Vanessa must have this hairbrush that's causing such a scene. And you gave Jamie such a wallop across the shoulder to get at her.

Mother tries to indicate his having extended his attack to another child, her attempt to calm the situation down, and, importantly, her realistic appraisal of the fact that her husband had hit the two other children, giving an indication that she had a greater sense of self-criticism, and sense of responsibility for things having gone wrong, that she is able to define what had occurred.

Father: I've played sports and if I want to hurt someone I can. And what I did, she was resting on the floor, lying on the floor, just in a very provocative pose and her arm was there, and I hit her with my foot, and her own hand went into her eye. Now they are the facts and I don't care what anybody says. And I mean this is the typically provocative way in which she distorts the truth, I kicked her in the face! . . . it's infuriating.

In this final statement father again reiterates the process which occurred and the fact that it was her hand that went into her eye, blaming her, rather than taking responsibility for his kicking action, even though as he indicated he could have done very serious damage.

In terms of the descriptive patterns for prognosis, this would be seen as a family with a doubtful prognosis, with a degree of uncertainty as to whether it could become a hopeful family situation. Doubt resides in the blaming and negative views of the girl by the father, who takes no responsibility for his aggressive act but sees it entirely as Vanessa's responsibility. The mother, on the other hand, is far more self-critical and feels far more responsible for things having gone wrong. Probably in an excessive way she has a great deal of personal distress related to her daughter's degree of handicap. This is clearly a self-maintaining system, and the issue arises as to whether they can accept a treatment contract.

The family was shocked when the therapeutic team insisted on linking with a child-protection agency, but they were able to accept the need for a period of therapeutic help, and Vanessa came into an in-patient unit which insisted on regular family sessions as part of the contract of admission. They were able to use therapeutic help involving the other two siblings as well as Vanessa and themselves. She was then able to return home when the issues had been dealt with: the pattern that led to abusive action and her own adolescent self-perception.

CHAPTER NINE

The treatment process in trauma-organized systems

T here has to be work with each individual involved in the trauma-organized system, as well as the system as a whole. Basically this involves work with the *victim* and work with the *victimizer*.

Work with the victim

There are two processes that have to be addressed:

1. Emotional processing.
2. Cognitive processing.

Emotional processing refers to work with the processes set in train by a traumatic event, e.g. the intrusive thoughts and re-experiencing; the avoidance phenomena of blanking out, deleting; and the arousal component which connects with anxiety, fear, and fight/ flight feelings. These processes need to be dealt with, which means being acknowledged, talked about, rehearsed in various ways in a supportive context. Instead of the reinforcement of fear, there needs to be re-experiencing in a context where support can be given, where integration can occur and a new reality and alternative story can emerge that can overcome the reality organized by the traumatic processes. Thus traumatic responses need to be "deconstructed" and appropriately protective responses constructed.

Cognitive processing describes the process by which explanations for the event, and its effect on ways of seeing and experiencing and giving meaning to relationships, can be reviewed. A reality and expectations can be developed that do not put the individual at risk.

The extent of treatment necessary will depend on the severity and extensiveness of the traumatic action and of the traumatic effect.

Work with the victimizer/abuser

A second core component to the work is work with the abuser. If work with the victim entails detailed exploration and sharing of experiences, in a facilitative, supportive environment, then the analogous process with the victimizer is a detailed examination of his or her abusive action. This needs to be carried out in a context of support and validation, rather than criticism. This then allows that individual to confront the way the abuse controls his life, and those close to him. He needs to examine the rationalizations, minimizations, and denials that surround the detailed abusive process, the sense of arousal, the transformation of anger to aggression whether physical, sexual, or emotional; the action itself in considerable detail; the feelings that accompany and follow the abusive action; the processing of the event, deletions, excitement, fantasies; the guilt, shame, arousal; and the re-emergence of abusive wishes and actions.

There are, of course variations in terms of whether the major violence is physical, sexual, or emotional; whether violent actions have become part of an addictive cycle, whether violent interactions involve more than one individual, within or outside the family. Abusive actions must thus be deconstructed and constructed so that caring, safe ways of relating can be developed, and can emerge. There is a similar need to be aware of emotional and cognitive processing of traumatizing, victimizing behaviour.

PUTTING THE WORK IN CONTEXT

Although work with victimizing and victim responses are the core elements for the individual, it is necessary to confront the fact that these elements may have to be dealt with in each individual. The "victim" may need help to avoid future abusive behaviour, e.g. in boys who may develop an abusive orientation as a defensive style. Victimizers construct their abuse on their own powerlessness. There is a consensus currently among therapists that work on victimizers' own abuse experiences needs to *follow* the "deconstruction" of their abusive behaviour, rather than preceding it. This then avoids the construction of further grievance and justification of abuse which can follow discussion of their own traumatic experiences.

There is an advantage for this work with individuals to occur in various contexts: with peers to counter feelings of aloneness and uniqueness, and for cross confrontation and support; with individuals to face experiences both as abuser and victim which feel "beyond" sharing; and within the family to acknowledge, share, accept responsibility, and give and receive support.

Work also needs to be done in the family and social context to clarify the nature and extent of abusive action and effect, and the protective capacity of those individuals not directly involved in traumatizing and victim actions. It is helpful to think of this work as involving a number of stages.

The first stage includes the discovery and breaking of the taboo of silence, when what may have been a long-standing violent pattern is revealed. During this phase the necessary assessment process has to be elaborated to determine how the abusive violent pattern can be stopped, how the individual victimized can be supported, whether the individual responsible for abusive actions can take responsibility, and whether there is a potential to work on the processes described previously. During this phase it is helpful to be able to acknowledge in the total family context that an abusive act has occurred, and to make a beginning to the open taking of responsibility, facing the minimizations and rationalizations, acknowledging the hurt, beginning the process of understanding the origin of the abuse, and viewing the factors that have maintained silence, that have facilitated abusive actions or secrecy.

The second stage is work during a phase when protection can be guaranteed to the victim, and a setting provided for the detailed work with all individual and family contexts. From the assessment period it will become clear whether a child can be protected and supported by a member of the family, or whether the child will need to be placed in a foster home or a therapeutic setting to initiate the work process. It may also become clear whether a couple can make a contract of safety, as described by Goldner and her colleagues, or whether a period of separation is needed; again the issue of responsibility—the acknowledgement of an abusing role—is an important part of this.

A variety of different ways of achieving emotional and cognitive re-processing need to be initiated relating to the particular set of problems and abusive patterns that are being re-enacted. Any or all of the following may be necessary:

- Individual work, or work in groups with individuals with similar traumatic experiences;

- work with individuals who have perpetrated similar violent acts;

- work with parents whose partners have abused their children;

- subsystem work, for instance to re-build or build a relationship between a care-taking parent and child that has been either damaged by abuse or has never been sufficiently strong

Where there is violence between a couple, a combination of individual and marital work may be necessary. Whole family sessions to help integrate shared new modes of seeing self and others will be necessary during this phase.

The third stage is rehabilitation. This is the stage that can be initiated once the processing during separation and in separate contexts has been achieved. It may then be possible to test whether a child can live within the original family context, or whether a couple can live safely together. During this phase there is a maximum need for whole family work; contexts need to be considered to assess whether this should be on a day or residential basis, or whether clinic attendance is sufficient.

The fourth stage is the new family context. Where it has proved impossible to achieve goals of providing adequate protection and a stage for the processing of victim and victimizing behaviour, then for a child a new family context may need to be confirmed. The child in foster care may require permanent adoption placement; other children may require longer periods of work within the therapeutic settings and the day and residential communities. This is necessary to help the child process his or her experiences sufficiently to be able to live within family contexts without enacting and re-enacting abusive patterns.

The incidence of abuse within foster and other caring contexts may be high, depending on the vulnerability of the child to re-enact, or the vulnerability of care-takers to the responses of particular children. The re-enactment by partners through interlocking choices of partners with similar characteristics is an additional risk associated with being involved with violent interactions, whether as child or partner.

THE ISSUE OF SOCIAL CONTROL

Social control is one of the most difficult issues in planning and carrying through treatment in cases of family violence. Without a mandate to carry through the treatment processes delineated earlier it is unlikely that treatment will be persisted with. Considerable resistance may need to be overcome to achieve the core essentials of emotional and cognitive processing for both victims and victimizers and a whole family context. Conversations about painful experiences and shameful actions have to occur against a background of a pull to denial, silence, and re-enactment rather than talking through.

Protection as the key principle

The principle that we have always used in the child abuse treatment programmes is that without a specific aim, it is unlikely that painful issues will be confronted. It could be argued that, once a child or family member becomes involved with a treatment programme, this in turn will create its own motivation. This is certainly an important factor, but inevitably the family has to get to the door. This means that therapeutic work must be a key to a child returning home, partners re-uniting, a parent having contact with a child.

The model developed has taken the protective agency as the key agency to be reported to by both family and therapeutic agency. We insist that all therapeutic work that involves more than one person—e.g. a meeting between a mother and children, a meeting between father and mother—should also include the protective agency built in as a constant validating pressure. It is a possible to say to a family member that "although I as a therapist could trust a partner or a parent, the issue is not what is going to convince me, but the social worker assigned to the protective role, and through her to her senior, and hence to the court standing as a societal force".

For instance, in an argument where a piece of work had been completed and we were planning for a 12-year-old to begin spending increasing amounts of time at home, the father asked in a challenging way why it was necessary to wait until half-term for the child to return home completely. I asked him what he thought the judge would say; for instance, would the judge want us to be taking a risk, even a small one, with his daughter, or would the judge wish us to be more cautious and ensure that each stage was taken at a pace where we could be as sure as possible she would be safe, and relationships could be seen to be working well? He responded, not surprisingly, that he would imagine the judge would want things to go fairly slowly and conservatively. We agreed, and the plan was arranged for her to return home at half-term.

Reporting to social control agencies

There are various ways in which this reporting and validating response can work. It is helpful to be able to ask in a group of abusive men what they would imagine I would need to know about them, and about the future situation, to be able to give a court a view that, for instance, contact would be possible with a child they had abused, or with a partner with whom there had been violent interaction. What would convince not me, but others, that the situation had really changed? What sort of change in attitude, what sort of "mission" of safety for others would have to be achieved to convince the court and society that the future could be different.

With one family we suggested that it might help a child protection case conference if they were to make a video in which they described and delineated the changes that had occurred. In this way the case conference could make the decision that, for instance, a stepfather who had been abusive to two of the daughters could begin to have further contact with his family. Interestingly, although the case conference members were indeed convinced and found the statements made within the family helpful, they still wanted assurance that *we* as the therapists were also convinced, so they could shift their responsibility onto us, or at least share it.

Ordinary confidentiality is not possible in such cases but can only be given in a relative way. For instance, when we meet with groups where there is no social worker representing the protective agency present, it is helpful to say that meetings are confidential, but that any issues that connect with the protection of a child will need to be reported. It is important to be able to convince external authorities that we—the men and ourselves—can report fully on the work that has been done and achieved. Another solution to this issue, described by Eileen Vizard and her team working in East London with convicted perpetrators, is to indicate that such meetings have *no* confidentiality. The content of group meetings is regularly reported to all other agencies and professionals on a need-to-know basis; thus protection issues are made the primary goal.

Can therapy be effective in an open system?

The question may arise as to whether therapy that takes place in such a closely monitored and reported context can be effective. Will there be real sharing, or only empty compliance and role playing?

It is helpful to have a number of different therapeutic contexts going on in parallel—e.g. as regular review meetings between professionals and family members, family members seen by different people in different settings—and an open network of communication. This very rapidly ensures that issues that are not being faced in one context can be picked up and brought back. The trauma-organized system—which attempts to silence, delete, and punctuate reality in particular ways—will be challenged and opened up if there are sufficient contexts and appropriate professionals to know family members, where they live, and how they relate.

There are cases where, for instance, it is discovered that a father who was supposed to be living separately from the family has been secretly in the family the whole time. These are almost always the cases where there was least openness, where there was a defensive refusal to take issues on board and confront them. It is essential to listen to "inner conversations" of discomfort and ask who in a family would be most likely to "give away" the fact of a parent not 'sticking to the rules".

Therapeutic sequences—abusers

In work with abusing individuals it is helpful to have a sequence of issues that have to be confronted and dealt with in an open way. It is useful to indicate that there is a programme which includes defining the cycle of abuse, defining attitudes towards children and women, understanding victim responses, and looking at their own victimization. At each of these steps there is almost inevitably a resistance to looking at such issues in detail.

The way that Jenkins (1990) has dealt with this, and which has proved helpful, is to create a *mission statement* for each man. This indicates that the aim is to confront and tackle the constraints from the past that have meant that instead of developing a caring, sensitive approach to women and children, they have become preoccupied with a set of fantasies and feelings of arousal which had led to deep-seated grievances and to regarding the child as a sexual object, not as a person. Taking this view makes it legitimate to say that each individual in the group needs to look in detail at exactly the way his abusive action occurred—what occurred before, what occurred afterwards, feelings, arousal, masturbatory fantasies—as part of a mission and as part of a goal and an aim to be safe in society.

One advantage of prosecution is that a therapist can offer to the court to take therapeutic responsibility for an offender, provided that a worker in the community, e.g. a probation officer, can assist, so that the man can live in society and continue to work. To be able to say that one has actually put one's own neck on the block to ensure that an abuser can live in the world rather than in prison is a powerful way of asking for something to be given in response—which is to face the unfaceable, the details of his own behaviour.

The group process—confrontation by other members of the group involved in the same process—is extremely valuable in achieving these goals and doing the very real work that needs to be achieved in delineating abusive cycles and taking control. The notion that this is a problem that can only be contained, handled, and avoided is a powerful message, similar to Bateson's notion of alcoholics having to accept defeat by the bottle.

Sequences of work with victim

With victims there may also be major issues with social control and therapeutic work, in the sense that on-going protection may be necessary. Often there is a tremendous wish not to be involved in therapeutic work. In family contexts there might be pressure to deny that abuse has occurred, to minimize and trivialize abusive experiences. A reality may be created in which the child has to agree that there are no problems, that there is no current distress, that that is all in the past.

It may be argued that bringing up the subject is just prolonging the agony and reminding the child of what he or she wishes to forget. The child may need to be asked whether he or she is always able to avoid thinking about past experiences, is never upset by a person who looks like or reminds them of the victimizer, that situations, places, are never reminders, that there are never flash-backs or moments between sleep and wake when memories surge back. In group work, very often children will say, "Oh, why do we have to speak about this again", or "You"ve made me speak about this again", with considerable irritation and anger, but obvious relief at re-processing and finding a different ending to their memories; in other words, speaking out rather than maintaining silence is valuable.

It is essential that therapeutic approaches acknowledge the fact that a "stressful" silence on the part of the therapist, intended to facilitate the child forward may have the reverse effect. Silence triggers off the memories of abuse, and the individual may not return. A positive out-going style of therapeutic work is essential; involvement in a series of different ways of approaching matters—e.g. through the use of videotapes, tasks, role-plays, art work, written work, etc.—are all necessary to engage children in the process.

Peer group experiences—bringing together children of similar ages, stages, and experiences—are helpful in reducing difference and in giving support. Themes that share details of experiences, understanding reasons, future scripts, self-protection, assertiveness are all helpful in the processing of trauma. Again the reporting to and the role of the protective agency is important. It is helpful for the social worker involved with a child to come with that child for joint meetings with therapeutic agencies to create a network so that issues of different stories and realities which may be created with different professionals or family members can be brought together in a consistent way.

Family work—sequences

A variety of different approaches to integrating the individual and group work can be used. There is a current debate about what issues are appropriate to work with in which context. Structural approaches are helpful in subsystem work to help a mother and traumatized child to learn to replace silence with conversations. Experiential methods, e.g. sculpting, can keep track of the origins of traumatizing relationships and the influence of new siblings or partners or relationships. Such methods can explore past and current patterns and a variety of new future possibilities.

Reflecting teams and co-therapy and network approaches all have their places in looking at processes that involve the multiple groups of various professionals and family members. However, conflict resolution by proxy needs to be kept in mind—e.g. the re-enactment of "victim" creating, by coming together, seeing our professional or family members as the "enemy", and recruiting others against them.

These issues can have powerful effects, blocking necessary emotional and cognitive processing.

Can family therapists be agents of social control and therapy and vice versa?

One question is, can the role of family therapist also include that of both a social control and a protection agent? This seems to be problematic. Although there is a major need for therapeutic authority to be able to confront and deal with painful issues in which there may be considerable pressure towards deletion and denial, it does seem problematic for the therapist, who may not have the powers or the authority, to provide a protective service as well.

On the other hand, protection agencies, e.g. Social Service departments, do have to carry through therapeutic pieces of work and be the protection agency at the same time. My own feeling is that this work could be maintained within an agency by the social worker using the authority of the agency through a colleague or senior to maintain social control whilst taking on a therapeutic role themselves. So that in the same way as saying to a family, "What would the court or social work agency require?", it would be possible for the social worker to ask what the senior managers, or the court, etc. would need to know, and need to be convinced about it, for the family to get the agencies off their back. The increasing role of courts may provide this notion of an authority to be related and reported to by a number of agencies.

The therapist may need to keep in mind a face towards the family, and a face towards the community that sanctions his professionalism.

It is to be hoped that legal developments, e.g. The Children Act (1989), with flexibility within its regulations, may assist professionals to create progressive partnerships. Authority and therapeutic work can also create a partnership with the family, a potential for conversation with the family enabling them to do the work which helps dissolve the trauma-organized system through changing their own ways of thinking, doing, and relating.

REFERENCES

Anderson, H., Goolishian, H., & Winderman, L. (1986). Problem determined systems toward transformation in family therapy. *Journal of Strategic & Systemic Therapies*, 5: 14–19.

Asen, K., George, E., Piper. R., & Stevens, A. (1989). A systems approach to child abuse: management and treatment issues. *Child Abuse & Neglect*, 13: 45–58.

Barratt, A., Trepper, T. S., & Fish, L. S. (1990). Feminist-informed family therapy for the treatment of intra-familial child sexual abuse. *Journal of Family Psychology*, 4: 151–166.

Bentovim, A., & Davenport, M. (1992). Resolving the trauma organised system of sexual abuse by confronting the abuser. *Journal of Family Therapy*, 14: 29–50.

Bentovim, A., & Kinston, W. (1991). Focal family therapy—joining systems theory with psychodynamic understanding. In: A. Gurman & D. Kniskern (Eds.), *Handbook for Family Therapy, Vol. 11*. New York: Basic Books.

Bograd, M. (1990). Why we need gender to understand human violence. *Journal of Interpersonal Violence*, 5: 132–135.

Burgess, R. L., & Conger, R. (1978). Family interactions in abusive, neglectful and normal families. *Child Development*, 49: 1163–1173.

Crittenden, P. (1988). Family and dyadic patterns of functioning in mal-treating families. In: K. Browne., C. Davies., & P. Stratten (Eds.), *Early Prediction and Prevention of Child Abuse.* Chichester: Wiley.

Dell, P. (1989). Violence and the systemic view: the problem of power. *Family Process, 28:* 1–14.

Dobash, R. E., & Dobash, R. (1979). *Violence against Wives.* New York: Free Press.

Egeland, B. (1988). Breaking the cycle of abuse. In: K. Browne, C. Davies, & P. Stratten (Eds.), *Early Prediction and Prevention of Child Abuse.* Chichester: Wiley.

Egeland, B., & Sroufe, A. (1981). Attachment and early maltreatment. *Child Development, 53:* 44–52.

Eth, S., & Pynoos, R.S. (Eds.) (1985). *Post-Traumatic Stress Disorder in Children.* Los Angeles: American Psychiatric Association.

Finklehor, D. (1984). *Child Sexual Abuse: New Theory and Research.* New York: Free Press.

Finklehor, D. (1987). The trauma of child sexual abuse: two models. *Journal of Interpersonal Violence, 2:* 348–366.

Furniss, T. (1983). Mutual influence and inter-locking professional fam-ily process in the treatment of child sexual abuse. *Child Abuse & Neglect, 7:* 207–223.

Gelles, R. J. (1987). *Family Violence* (second edition). London: SAGE.

George, C., & Main, M. (1979). Social interactions of young abused children: approach, avoidance and aggression. *Child Development, 50:* 306–318.

Goldner, V., Penn, P., Sheinberg, M., & Walker, G. (1990). Love and violence: gender paradoxes in volatile attachments. *Family Process, 29:* 343–365.

Hodges, G. (1991). *The Use of Story Stems to Assess Attachments in Chil-dren.* Presentation. London: Institute of Child Health.

Jenkins, A. (1990). *Invitations to Responsibility.* Adelaide: Dulwich Centre Publications.

Kinston, W. (1987). *A General Theory of Symptom Formation.* (Unpub-lished).

Kinston, W., & Bentovim, A. (1980). Creating a focus for brief marital and family therapy. In: S. H. Budmann (Ed.), *Forms of Brief Therapy.* New York: Guilford Press.

Kinston, W., & Bentovim, A. (1990). A framework for family descrip-tion. *Journal of Contemporary Family Therapy, 12:* 279–297.

Kinston, W., Loader, P., & Miller, L. (1987). Quantifying the clinical assessment of family health. *Journal of Marital and Family Therapy, 13*: 49–67.

Loader, P., Burck, C., Kinston, W., & Bentovim, A. (1981). Method for organising the clinical description of family interaction: the family interaction format. *Australian Journal of Family Therapy, 2*: 131–141.

Maccoby, E. E., & Martin, J. A. (1983). Socialisation in the context of the family: parent/child interaction. In: E. M. Hetherington (Ed.), *Handbook of Child Psychology, Vol. IV*. New York: John Wiley.

Madonna, P., Scoyk, S., & Jones D. T. (1991). Family interaction within incest and non-incest families. *American Journal of Psychiatry, 5* (Part 1): 46–49.

McNeely, R. L., & Mann, C. R. (1990). Domestic violence is a human issue. *Journal of Interpersonal Violence, 5*: 129–132.

Main, M. (1991). *A Typology of Human Attachment Organisation, Assessed in Discourse, Drawings and Interviews*. Cambridge: Cambridge University Press.

Monck, E., Bentovim, A., Goodall, G., Hyde, C., Lwin, R., & Sharland, S. (1991). *Child Sexual Abuse: A Descriptive and Treatment Study*. Research Report from Institute of Child Health, Hospitals for Sick Children, London, to the Department of Health.

Mullen, P. E., Romans-Clarkson, S., Walton, D. A., & Herbison, G. P. (1988). Impact of sexual and physical abuse on women's mental health. *Lancet, 1648*: 841–845.

Oppenheimer, R., Howells, K., Palmer, R. L., & Chaloner, D. A. (1985). Adverse sexual experience in childhood and clinical eating disorders: a preliminary description. *Journal of Psychiatric Research, 19*: 356–361.

Seligman, M. E. P. (1975). *Helplessness: On Depression, Development and Death*. San Francisco: Freeman.

Stratton, P., & Swaffer, R. (1988). Maternal casual beliefs for abused and handicapped children. *Journal of Reproductive and Infant Psychology, 6*: 201–216.

Strauss, M. A., & Gelles, R. J. (1987). Is violence towards children increasing? In: R. J. Gelles (Ed.), *Family Violence* (second edition). London: SAGE.

Strauss, M. A., & Kantor, G. K. (1987). Stress and child abuse. In: R. E. Helfer & R. S. Kemp (Eds.), *The Battered Child* (fourth edition). Chicago: University of Chicago Press.

Sylvester, J. (1990). *Attributions of Parents Who Abuse Their Children.* Ph.D. Dissertation, University of Leeds.

Terr, L. (1991). Child traumas: an outline and overview. *American Journal of Psychiatry, 148*: 10–20.

Vizard, E., & Tranter, M. (1988). Helping young children to describe experiences of child sexual abuse—general issues. In: A. Bentovim, A. Elton, J. Hilderbrand, M. Tranter, & E. Vizard (Eds.), *Child Sexual Abuse within the Family.* London: Butterworths/Wright.

White, M. (1989). *The Externalising of the Problem and the Re-authoring of Lives and Relationship.* Dulwich Centre Newsletter. Adelaide: Dulwich Centre Publications.

White, M., & Epston, D. (1989). *Literate Means to Therapeutic Ends.* Adelaide: Dulwich Centre Publications.

INDEX